my neighbor don't talk too good

Wally Metts

ACCENT BOOKS

MEMBER OF
EVANGELICAL CHRISTIAN
PUBLISHERS ASSOCIATION

ACCENT BOOKS
A division of Accent-B/P Publications
12100 W. Sixth Avenue
P.O. Box 15337
Denver, Colorado 80215

Copyright © 1978 Accent-B/P Publications, Inc.
Printed in U.S.A.

Library of Congress Number: 78-69762

ISBN 0-89636-005-9

**Dedicated to
Rev. Richard E. Riley
and
Dr. Bruce P. Lackey**

Whose friendship has remained steadfast in spite of my frequent eccentricities and my failure to adequately respond in kind for the ample benefits their lives have bestowed upon me.

CONTENTS

PREFACE

Twenty years ago I laid down my hammer and paint brush and set out on a course in which my livelihood and activities would be engaged almost exclusively with my ability to use the spoken word. The years have not disappointed me. It has pleased the Lord to permit my words to open doors for me to travel into every section of this great nation and abroad. I now have friends in every section of the United States and around the world. The years have been extremely good to my family and me. We have been well fed, clothed and educated. We have been adequately cared for financially. We have experienced untold blessings. Best of all, we have had the unspeakable privilege of having a part in the service of the King.

Frankly, I am amazed at the power of words. I sincerely believe they hold the key to a new plateau of experience for anyone who cares to explore their power. In the following meditations I hope to whet your appetite for discovering the remarkable power that lies in the world of words.

—Wally Metts

Chapter One

MY NEIGHBOR
DON'T TALK TOO GOOD

Over a period of three years, I had been trying to communicate to my neighbors my position in a thorny boundary problem. Letters had been exchanged, talks had been held in friendly, informal sessions and phone calls had been frequent and cordial.

Yet, three years later, there they were. Representatives from two households were standing in my driveway wanting to know more clearly what I had meant in my last phone call. They had even consulted a lawyer! I reiterated once again, as clearly as I could, my plans, assuring them that I did not intend to take any action that would be mean, despiteful or harmful to them. A friendly agreement was reached and all of us felt relieved that the problem had been solved. Or had it? Was I able to get through to them, or would the situation come up again? Would there be another misunderstanding? One of my neighbors had said, "We just need to get together and talk these things over." But we had talked them over time and again, and still I had been misunderstood. My little daughter used to say, "I misunderheard you!"

Maybe the time would arise when the situation would get more serious. Would my neighbors be able to say, "We tried to work this thing out, but my neighbor don't talk too good?" The implication is obvious. My accuser would be a little derelict in his speech, too.

Immediately we would take note of his grammar. We would say that he doesn't speak too well himself. But communication is more than using proper English and knowing how to put a sentence together. My business is communication. Words are my stock in trade, yet I had failed repeatedly to make myself understood by my neighbors. I wondered how many times I had said things from the pulpit that were completely misunderstood, or failed in getting across the idea that had been intended.

The title for this book may seem a bit

zany, but there is more truth reflected in its obviously garbled grammar that most of us would suspect. How well are you communicating with your neighbors? With your friends? With your family? Is the problem all on their side? Or is it partly on your side?

Poor communication can be costly. A close family member recently came very near losing a valuable teaching job. The problem arose over a breakdown in communications between him and a board member. Every day jobs are lost, families are hurt, marriages are broken and churches are split because of the difficulty of "talking things over." We gradually learn how to make sounds, then form words as small children. But many of us grow to adulthood without ever learning to *communicate*. Nor is it a problem of language alone. It is also a *spiritual* problem. The Lord told Moses: "If a soul sin, and commit a trespass against the Lord, and lie unto his neighbor in that which was delivered him to keep, or in fellowship, or in a thing taken away by violence, or hath deceived his neighbour..." (Leviticus 6:2).

Here we learn, among other things, that sinning and trespassing against the Lord includes the way we communicate with our neighbors. Jesus had some very pointed things to say about how we treat our neighbors in the summation of the law and prophets (Matthew 22:37-40), the parable of the Good Samaritan and the Golden Rule. With most of us it is not a question of whether we will punch our neighbor in the nose. With most of us it is a question of how or whether we will talk to him.

If the way we talk to others is a matter of vital concern to God, and if the failure to do so properly is a sin against Him, is there any chance that Satan, that arch deceiver, might be interested in jamming the signal and fouling up our communications with our spouses, our friends, our business associates and our fellow church members? How many lives can he foul up? How many people can he deceive by garbling the day-by-day conversation of the average Joe or Jane? Can he accomplish his ends by making Joe misunderstand Jane? Is it only the words of the Scriptures he wants us to be deceived about, or can he deceive us spiritually by using communication failure to put conflict, bitterness and apathy into our lives?

These are some of the questions I have set out to answer in this book. While I don't profess to have advanced very far in exploring Bible principles of communication, I think I have discovered some vital principles that can change your world by making you aware of the dynamic power of words.

To begin with, I want to look at some problems that contribute to the failure to accurately share ideas—in other words, some things that can cause your neighbor to think you "don't talk too good."

THINGS THAT BLOCK COMMUNICATION

Talking, writing and other forms of communication are the glue that holds the world together. If we could not reach out and exchange ideas with those around us, this would be a strange world. What a tragic picture we see in those poor, withdrawn people who so fear life and its consequences they cut themselves off from the world, draw into a shell and refuse to talk. It is healthy and desirable to talk to other people, to learn from them and to work together on the problems that surround all of us. God invented human language, and in doing so gave us a valuable tool for survival.

While the following unhealthy blocks to effective communication do not at all exhaust the list of things that happen to cut off our relationship to others, they at least give us a start. All of them are recognized in the Scriptures, though we will not take time here to cite specific verses.

PRECONCEIVED BIAS

Call it prejudice, preconceived ideas, a bent toward a singular thought—it all adds up to the same thing. Sometimes we are on a different channel. We have an idea locked in our heads, and all the signals in the world cannot burst through our consciousness to introduce a contrary idea. Whether approaching the Scriptures with an unbendable idea that refuses to be changed or stubbornly holding on to our side of a family argument, it is a result of the same thing, a bent view. And it breaks down communication. The circuits are jammed. No new idea can come through. Bias binds communication.

BLIND SPOTS

All of us have things about ourselves which our fellows know better than we do. It may be a fatal flaw in our character or a besetting weakness. And when our communication with others touches on that blind spot, we break down in our ability to understand what is being said. We simply cannot see it. We may be able to see the same thing if it shows up in another person, but we refuse to see it in ourselves. It stops communication because we are incapable of receiving any further information on the matter. We are blind to it.

EMOTIONAL FIRE

When anger, loyalty, intense love, commitment to a cause or other emotional factors enter into the communication problem, they often short-circuit reason. The tongue ceases to be an imparter of ideas and becomes a fire. James, in fact, says "The tongue is a fire" (James 3:6). Let a ruler become aroused and he will call up his followers with an appeal to loyalty, and war will begin. Armies rally around the commands of men, thus the culprit is often the tongue. Hitler, by means of volatile speeches, fired his followers to unbelievable zeal for an unholy cause.

Let a family become divided and the emotions take over. Both sides take up the side of the one nearest to them. It does not matter that somebody on the other side might be making better sense; it is not the communication of ideas but blind love and loyalty that rule. The fire burns away the wires of communication.

EMOTIONAL SCARS

Long after the fires have gone out, the scars left by the fire remain. Some people have been so hurt, so scarred by the fray they will suffer communication problems for years. When this is true, there are some subjects one dare not bring up for fear they will only renew the hurt or recall the conflict. In his dealings with others, the Christian, especially, should remember that if he is not coming through to others he may be dealing with those who are carrying scars that only the grace of God can heal. Healing the hurts of others is a vastly important business for us to be in.

LACK OF SKILL IN SPEAKING

At times, our failure to be understood or to understand others, is simply a lack of skill in speaking. Since Moses and Paul both seemed to possess that problem, it is no mark of ignorance. Not everyone possesses verbal skills. And even those who do have some skill may not possess it equally in all areas. Paul's speech in person was said to be "contemptible," while his letters were considered "weighty and powerful" (II Corinthians 10:10). We know his letters were powerful, since many of them make up part of the New Testament. But in reading his letters, how many of us would judge his speech as being contemptible?

In recognizing a difference of skill in the ability to communicate, we can often keep from making the rash judgment, "My neighbor don't talk too good!"

DESIRE FOR PRIVACY

Why does the film star sometimes become angry with a news photographer, or the millionaire sometimes become a recluse? It is frequently because they grow impatient of being so much in the public eye and want relief from it. In varying degrees, all of us place a premium on our privacy. Our thoughts can be very private things too. There are times when we have difficulty communicating with others because they do not want to expose their thoughts. This type of person is thought of as unfriendly, or shy. In reality, they may only be reluctant to share their thoughts with others until they are sure they can be trusted. The Bible even encourages this kind of behavior (Proverbs 21:23).

PERSONAL OFFENSE

Sometimes a failure to be understood results from having previously offended our hearer. We may not even know it. This type of case is difficult to overcome: "A brother offended is harder to be won than a strong city: and their contentions are like the bars of a castle" (Proverbs 18:19). Until the basic offense is resolved, ideas and thoughts cannot be shared because the offense has built something that is "like the bars of a castle."

SATANIC INTERFERENCE

The two main tactics of Satan are to accuse and to deceive. They both work together. Think of the following example: A member of a certain family becomes a Christian. He immediately has a desire for other family members to experience the joy he has come to know. He sets about to let them know how Christ can make the difference for them, too. How can Satan stop him? Easy. He can create a misunderstanding. Once he can attach a wrong motive, or take a word out of context, or otherwise foul up the signal, he can instantly stop the message. The words of the well-meaning Christian no longer have any effect, since the meaning has been effectively blocked by a misunderstanding.

These little misunderstandings are often no less dangerous than the spreading of a heresy by a false religious cult. Satan does not care how he does it as long as he can block the message. If he can do it by creating strife and misunderstanding among family members and friends, he has often hurt more than he could through the agency of a false teacher who might be considered more neutral.

Suppose a group of Christians is living in a victorious manner, and those around them are beginning to notice that there is something different and real about them. How can Satan stop such effective witness? Simple. He can cause a misunderstanding that turns brother against brother, thus effectively destroying their influence. It is no small thing when this happens. It touches many lives who otherwise could have been influenced for Christ.

In the following pages, we are going to investigate some of the problems and possibilities involved in the world of words. We hope to be able to assist some readers in coming to the place where they can "talk good."

Chapter Two

WORDS THAT WOUND

Slander is "a false statement harmful to another's character or reputation." It can contain an element of truth and still be slander, if it conveys an untrue impression. Whenever a witness is placed on the stand in a courtroom, the opposing lawyer is given the privilege of cross-examination. The trained counselor knows that a word here and there, taken out of context, can give a false picture of the facts as they really are. A lawyer realizes that a witness can piece together a number of true statements in such a way that the entire sum of those statements is a lie because of the impression it leaves. They also know that a witness can speak a number of true things, omitting other true things, and create a fabrication because of the omissions that otherwise could shed the true light on the facts.

In cautioning us about what we say of others, God uses the example of a witness in formal proceedings. In the ninth commandment, He says, "Thou shalt not bear false witness against thy neighbour" (Exodus 20:16). It is our total statement, the sum of the words we speak concerning our neighbor that He has in mind. So concerned is He about how we speak about others, Jesus says in Matthew 18:15,16: "Moreover if thy brother shall trespass against thee, go and tell him his fault between thee and him alone: if he shall hear thee, thou hast gained thy brother. But if he will not hear thee, then take with thee one or two more, that in the mouth of two or three witnesses every word may be established."

Judges and lawyers have to be very careful about procedure. Our system of jurisprudence is outlined in such a way that built-in safeguards protect the accused from being falsely charged with an uncommitted crime. Although some miscarriages of justice still occasionally occur, we must wonder how much better off all of us would be if the same care were exercised in our ordinary conversation about our neighbors and friends!

STEALING A PRECIOUS POSSESSION

I wonder how many of us have really

pondered the words in Proverbs 22:1: "A good name is rather to be chosen than great riches, and loving favour rather than silver and gold." A person's name is a precious thing. Whenever we hear mention of a name, our thoughts naturally turn to the person who owns it. During the Watergate affair, names that were synonymous with public service were suddenly tainted with corruption. Many people, though innocent of charges, had to undergo the trauma of guilt by association.

All of us cherish the thoughts that are associated with our names. We want people to think well of us. "Reputation" is the word that describes how people associate good or ill with our names. If I damage a person's name, I have stolen something from him that is very valuable. People put such high value on names in ancient times that parents chose names with special meanings, marking some important event or hoping to guide their children into some virtuous path by giving them a name to live up to.

God also puts a premium on our names. Our identity is so valuable to Him that He has given us a special promise of a new name (Revelation 2:17). There is a sense in which we are whatever our names are, since the mention of our name calls to the minds of others everything we are in their sight. In His care to see that our names are protected, God has taken unusual precautions to safeguard our reputations.

It is a sad commentary on our profane age that many of our journalists are so hungry for money they take little care for a person's name. The type of character assassination we hear on every hand goes hand in hand with unbridled violence. They both are equally injurious and sinful. All of us need to know what precautions can be taken to protect the good names of those around us.

THE SPIRIT OF ACCUSATION

Speaking of names, both "Satan" and "devil" mean "accuser." Satan's whole method is to accuse, to slander. In Genesis 3 we see him accusing God to man. In the book of Job we see him accusing man to God. In Matthew 4 we see him accusing the God-man. In speaking of Satan's fall, John said, "For the accuser of our brethren is cast down, which accused them before our God day and night" (Revelation 12:10). You can see what kind of company we are in when we go into the accusing business!

HOW TO BE A GOOD REPORTER

On the other hand, a good reporter is objective and careful in reporting the facts. And he is in business to inform his readers rather than victimize his subjects. God is interested in good reports. Of faith He declared, "For by it the elders obtained a good report" (Hebrews 11:2). And of pastors He required, "Moreover he must have a good report of them which are without" (I Timothy 3:7). One of the strengths of a godly pastor is that he enjoys a good reputation among those on the outside of the church. How many pastors have had their ministries rendered ineffective by the careless talk of some vicious tongue!

It is no less important for anybody else to avoid accusatory speech. Young people frequently have their lives wrecked when hateful tales steal one of their most precious possessions—their reputations. When we hear something about another person that is unfavorable to his reputation, the damage done by remaining silent is not one tenth that done by carelessly repeating a "morsel" that might rob him of his good name! By carelessly repeating an unproven and unnecessary thought about another, we send emotional and spiritual forces crashing down around his head that are "curses" in every sense of the word.

In order to protect the sanctity involved in another person's good name, God has outlined instructions we must follow in order to be good reporters.

TELL HIM ALONE

What is my duty if someone comes to

me speaking of the offensive act of another? My first duty is not to listen unless the reporter has talked to the person in question. To every bit of gossip, I could well answer, "Before I listen, let me ask you a question. Have you gone to that person and discussed it with him? It could very well be that you have misunderstood the situation. I have been commanded by the Scriptures not to listen to a report like this unless certain precautions are taken, in order to protect the reputation of other people."

It can readily be seen that a lot of unkind remarks about others would evaporate under such precautions. This is exactly what Jesus commanded in Matthew 18: "Moreover if thy brother shall trespass against thee, go and tell him his fault between thee and him alone" (verse 15). Jesus is saying any real or imagined trespass is to be kept quiet until we discuss it alone with the person involved. Any good reporter knows that a good report involves going straight to the source. It is amazing how twisted a story can get by the time it passes through several sets of ears! Courts have a word for that: They call it *hearsay*.

ASK WHERE THE WITNESSES ARE

If the person telling the story were to come back to me later and say, "Well, I went to him and talked it over. It didn't do any good. Now, let me tell you what he did," would I be free to listen? Not according to the Scriptures. Something is still lacking. Listen to the next precaution: "But if he will not hear thee, then take with thee one or two more, that in the mouth of two or three witnesses every word may be established" (Matthew 18:16). Like a court of law, I must have witnesses. As in justice proceedings, if the word is not established "in the mouth of two or three witnesses," it is tantamount to bearing false witness against my neighbor.

After discussing the proceedings necessary in church disciplinary action, our Lord goes on to say: "Verily I say unto you, Whatsoever ye shall bind on earth shall be bound in heaven: and whatsoever ye shall loose on earth shall be loosed in heaven" (Matthew 18:18). The reason why what we say in the cases of offending people is so important is that it has an effect in Heaven as well as on earth. There are spiritual powers extant in the universe which are affected by our words. We can bind and loose.

Our whole purpose in life should be to loose, to unshackle others from the spiritual chains that bind them. Much more loosing could be done if we were to talk *to* others before we talk *about* them. In the book of Galatians, for example, Paul takes up the subject of how to act toward an offending brother: "Brethren, if a man be overtaken in a fault, ye which are spiritual, restore such an one in the spirit of meekness; considering thyself, lest thou also be tempted" (Galatians 6:1).

Notice that the whole emphasis of this passage is that we are not to *accuse* but to *restore*. It is Satan who came to accuse, but Jesus who came to restore. Whether or not we slander depends entirely upon our attitude toward others. If we are out to "get" them, we will repeat anything about them we hear, so eager are we to justify our feelings toward them. But if they say something about a friend, our first impulse is to say, "I just can't believe that!" In the one case we are an accuser, in the other a restorer.

It is often the creation of an image among others that forces people deeper into a life of wrongdoing. We cannot divorce ourselves from our images. Often, in aiding in the assault on another's reputation, we are forcing them into a corner in which they are cut off from the kind of good companions who can help them, and open only to those who will help them justify that bad reputation. In this sense we are "binding" them both on earth and in Heaven. By seeking to restore, on the other hand, we can bring them into the kind of company they need.

The prophet Nathan is a good example of how to restore. After David's terrible sin there were, no doubt, those who delighted in attacking his reputation. But not Nathan. He went directly to David, the person in question. After telling the parable of a rich man who stole the only ewe of a poor man, Nathan confronted the King of Israel with an image that was uncomfortable to him. "Thou art the man," the prophet thundered. (II Samuel 12:7). And although a number of drastic consequences followed David's sinful actions, David was restored when the prophet told him "alone."

Even the truth can be told with a design to hurt. The difference between slander and restoration lies in our motive. If we are trying to hurt, we will use the truth to slander. If we are trying to help, we will use it to restore.

How sweet our names are to us! It helps to remember that others have the same regard for their names. The wise person will help to protect another's name.

Chapter Three

A WORLD OF WORDS

One day God walked out and looked at the edge of nothing. Then He began to speak. Whatever He said came true. He told the planets, the elements, the stars and the earth to appear. His words became worlds. Millenniums later, science has concluded that all matter and space are composed of forms of energy. It is energy that sustains it and holds it in the intricate little universes which make up all matter. God's Word is that energy.

While *our* words have not nearly so much effect upon the physical world, our words have a profound effect upon *our* world. God says the world is not built upon the foundation of atoms and molecules, but upon the principle of truth and wisdom: "The Lord by wisdom hath founded the earth; by understanding hath he established the heavens" (Proverbs 3:19).

THE WORLD SPEAKS

God designed the world in such a way as to point men to Himself. Every part of His creation is a reflection of His glory and power. Language, far from arising from the first few faltering grunts of a caveman, was invented by God Himself, and was given to us to communicate with one another and with Him. One of the first acts of Adam following his creation was to name the animals, and we can be sure he gave them names with much meaning. As he walked among the trees of the garden, Adam received wisdom and instruction from the creation. While here on earth, Jesus had the power to command the wind, call up a fish with money in its mouth and even call the dead out of the grave. While it is not suggested that any man except Christ ever had such power, it is possible that His power reflected some power lost in the fall. Man was given dominion over the earth and its creatures and it is possible that involved the ability to command certain elements of the creation.

What is true of the physical world is true also of the spiritual world. Think of the world you live in. It is made up of physical components, to be sure. We are usually preoccupied with the house we live in, the car we drive, the material possessions we enjoy. But our world is more than that. It is a world of communication. Think of a world in which nobody talked! Ours is a world of arguments, exchanges of love, the search for new ideas. A house would not be much of a house with nobody to talk to. A car would be less appealing without friends at each destination.

When God gave you the power to speak, He gave you a certain amount of control over your world. Chances are, the paycheck you enjoy came your way because you used words wisely in asking for a job. Your words, then, have been translated into money. When you get your money, you use language to translate your money into whatever you wish to exchange it for. Everywhere we turn, we live in a world of words. And knowing how to use words plays a vital role in the way you control, or are controlled by, your world.

Most of us underestimate the role language plays. But how many words do you imagine you speak in a day, from that first grunt in the morning to the last groan at night? You handle more words in a few minutes than dollars in a week. Words flow endlessly from us, to us, around us and even above us. Our families, our friends, our fellow employees, our customers, our churches all shower us constantly with words. We drown in a sea of paper that reaches us each day in our mailboxes. The telephone rings off the hook at the most inappropriate times. We scan the newspapers, soothe our wives, send the kids off to the backyard and shout at the dog. The neighbor wants to borrow the lawnmower. The bills inform us of how much we owe. The television blares away between radio announcements. Words, words, words. We live in a world of words!

SNARES AND SWORDS

The subject of words is so important that the book of Proverbs is filled with warnings and promises about how we control our world with words. For instance, if a person becomes a surety for a loan, Proverbs 6:2 says: "Thou art snared with the words of thy mouth, thou art taken with the words of thy mouth." Proverbs 12:13 warns, "The wicked is snared by the transgression of his lips." God says our words are traps we can fall into. How many of us can count times when we have trapped ourselves with our own words!

But our words are said to be not only traps, but also weapons, as we see in Proverbs 12:18: "There is that speaketh like the piercings of a sword." In Proverbs 18:8 and 26:22 we read: "The words of a talebearer are as wounds." Think of the times you have been wounded with words! And think of the times you have wounded others. The tongue is a weapon, much like a loaded gun. And we must take care not to hurt anyone with our weapon, the tongue.

Thankfully, words have the power not

only to hurt but to heal as well. Proverbs 12:18 continues, "The tongue of the wise is health." Each of us has the power in our grasp to heal others. We can affect our whole world by bringing healing to people through our words.

So our words are not simply harmless little things that evaporate like so much vapor. They are substantive, powerful and world-changing. There is hardly any way to overestimate the potential words have for changing your life.

A tall, gangling man with a stovepipe hat fidgeted nervously one day as he rode on a train. He was straining over a scrap of brown paper on which he was writing a few words to say at a memorial service. We call these words the *Gettysburg Address*. A nation rode out one of its most difficult periods on the wings of those words.

A fiery young man stood in a small church building one night and challenged, "Is peace so sweet or life so dear as to be purchased at the price of chains and slavery? Forbid it, Almighty God! I know not what course others may take. But as for me, give me liberty or give me death!" A revolution was borne upon those words that changed the world's view of what governments should be like.

Words are a life and death matter, as revealed in the book of Proverbs: "Death and life are in the power of the tongue: and they that love it shall eat the fruit thereof" (Proverbs 18:21).

Words are worth money. Sponsors pay millions of dollars for a few minutes on television to get their message out to the public. Radio preachers pay money to have the privilege of sending out words over the air. Authors are paid for their words on the printed page. In fact, a few men have become fabulously wealthy by putting their words down on paper in an instructive or entertaining way. The influence certain newsmen and entertainers exert upon the world by their words is almost beyond imagination. But, as important as all this is, there is a world of even greater importance.

OUR LINK WITH
THE SPIRITUAL WORLD

The book of James tells us that words are the elements of power in the spiritual world: "And the tongue is a fire, a world of iniquity: so is the tongue among our members, that it defileth the whole body, and setteth on fire the course of nature; and it is set on fire of hell" (James 3:6).

Think for a moment. What is our link with the spiritual world? When God wants to have contact with us, what does He do? He speaks to us. It may be through the pages of His Word, or by His Word in that "still, small, voice." If we want to have contact with God, what do we do? We read our Bibles or pray. It is all based upon communication, on the art of language, on words.

When Satan approached Eve, what did he use? Words! He spoke to her. If Satan was communicating then, is he still speaking? How is he speaking? Is he speaking through today's literature, communications media, educational institutions and philosopher-scientists? How is he affecting you and me through what he is saying?

We know there is a global warfare between great spiritual forces. But most of us do not realize that the gigantic struggle is being waged in a world of words. We passively, almost casually, let these words flood in upon us, little realizing what they are doing to our world. If the tongue is "set on fire of hell," as James says, what of the almost ceaseless barrage of words coming to us every moment through unconverted men of destitute character, twisted philosophy and unrealistic world view? Is it harmless, or is it an attack by Satan?

We talk about spiritual power, whether good or evil. Power has to have a conductor of some kind. What is it that carries spiritual power? It is words. And who carries the words that contain the spiritual power? People—the man at the market, the man on the radio, the woman at the club, the teacher at the school, the salesman, the ad writer. Young people are deceived, lives are ruined and people go to Hell because of the terrible potential of words for spiritual power. On the other hand, harlots are made pure, drunkards are reclaimed and sins are forgiven through the power of words.

We live not only in a material world, but also in an unseen spiritual world. The dynamic of that spiritual world is in the ability to speak. Whatever your spiritual condition at this moment, it has been determined by your reception of, or indifference to, words.

In the spiritual battle we are engaged in, the battlefield is the mind. And the entrance to the mind is through words. From the very beginning, we learn important lessons through words. "Yes" and "no" are the simple words an infant soon comprehends to mean that there is authority in the world. "Daddy" and "Mommy" are words that indicate there is love. From this simple beginning our world is shaped by words.

The ultimate authority is God. He also has His "yes" and "no." The moment we turn His "yes" into a "no," and His "no" into a "yes," we experience the jarring discord of sin. Sin is rebellion against the gracious command of God. From that moment on, our will is pitted against His will and we go our own way. But He doesn't leave us alone.

He has caused His mind and His will to be written down for us to read. It is the Book we call the Bible. In it God tells us there are things He wants us to do, informs us that we haven't done them, and describes the remedy for our rebellion. But rebellious man will have none of it. He still wants to do his own thing. So through His preachers, in the message of creation, over radio stations, through the printed page, and in an almost endless variety of ways, God is calling out to His rebellious creature to return.

But there is another message out there besides God's. Any message that ignores the Bible, makes light of the reality of God, lures into a path of transgression or otherwise departs from the message of truth and the gospel is a false message, causing the most dire consequences. There is a constant struggle of the will, a tug-of-war between opposing forces. And the thing that pulls is the terrible spiritual reality of words!

Chapter Four

RECAPTURING A FORGOTTEN POWER

The godly old patriarch, Jacob, had thought for years that his son, Joseph, was dead. But in his old age he had discovered not only that Joseph was alive, but that he was second in command over the government of Egypt. Shortly thereafter Jacob and his sons migrated to Egypt, and settled in the land of Goshen where, at length, the time came for the old man to prepare for his death. One of those preparations was to bless his descendants, as his father had done for him and his brother Esau. One by one his sons came before him as he put his hands upon them and uttered the remarkable blessings that outlined the next few centuries of Jewish history (Genesis 49). There were no presents in his hands. His words were his gifts. But in some way those words of blessing contained the remarkable power to grant favor and control the course of events.

Of course Jacob was not the only one in the Bible whose words were powerful. Much later in Israel's history, Elijah stood in Naboth's vineyard and pronounced a curse upon Ahab and Jezebel. Isaiah loosed a verbal shaft from Heaven that resulted in the death of the hordes of Sennacherib's army. Elisha spoke words that blinded an army, and called down fire from heaven upon two companies of his tormenters. The false prophet, Balaam, was hired by Balak to curse Israel, although God prevented him from doing it.

In the New Testament, the disciples used the name of Jesus to bring healing, cast out devils and open prisons by the power of the spoken word. While the Bible does reveal that certain unusual periods of miraculous activity were in operation during those times, nevertheless the general principle remains: Our words have a potential that men usually do not dream of.

DO WE HAVE THE SAME POWER TODAY?

In the field of education we have discovered that some children have learning problems as a direct result of their parents' methods of talking to them. Has God included in the power of parenthood the ability to bind or set free merely by what we say to our children? Do we have the ability to visualize certain futures for our children and speak prophecies that become self-fulfilling?

I have preached in churches where the Spirit of God did not seem to be working although the pastor and certain people were really serving the Lord and trying to do His work. In examining the situation, I found a substantial number of people in the congregation who were saying in effect, "It can't be done here." Are people able to build spiritual fences around their leaders by their words, cutting off the power that would otherwise be available to them? Even Jesus, returning to His hometown, was not able to exercise His power because of the lack of faith in the people around Him. They were saying words like, "Is not this the carpenter?" (Mark 6:1-6).

I have known men with great potential who were absolutely defeated because they were saying, "I guess I'm just no good!"

What is the connection between our words and our faith? What can we do to regain the forgotten power to be mighty with words?

THE GOD KIND OF FAITH

In one of the most graphic scenes in the New Testament, Jesus laid down a principle for His disciples that is capable of changing your whole frame of reference about the world around you. Early on the morning following His triumphant procession into Jerusalem, He and His disciples started out once again from Bethany to Jerusalem. They soon came upon a fig tree, and Jesus walked over to it as if to eat some of its fruit. Finding the early leaf on it, but no fruit, He cursed it. It seems to be such an insignificant happening at first. But, the next day, upon returning by the place, the disciples saw that it was withered. Peter commented on it, and the Lord made a significant and startling observation:

Have faith in God [literally, "the faith of God," or "the God kind of faith"]. For verily I say unto you, That whosoever shall say unto this mountain, Be thou removed, and be thou cast into the sea; and shall not doubt in his heart, but shall believe that those things which he saith shall come to pass; he shall have whatsoever he saith. Therefore I say unto you, What things soever ye desire, when ye pray, believe that ye receive them, and ye shall have them.

Mark 11:22-24

In carefully reading this passage, two things come to our attention. The first is a principle, the next is an application. The principle is expressed in verses 22,23: "Have faith in God . . . whosoever shall say unto this mountain, Be thou removed . . . and shall not doubt in his heart . . . he shall have whatsoever he saith." The principle here is that a person with a certain kind of faith—the God kind of faith—can talk to a mountain, order its removal, and have what he says! That the principle is not confined to the act of prayer is seen in the fact that the person in question is talking to a mountain. We do not pray to mountains. The passage is saying that if we can connect ourselves to the available power of God by a vital, real faith, that faith can translate the power of God in and through our spoken word!

Having laid down the principle, Jesus makes His application to our prayer lives in verse 24, connecting the two together with the word, "therefore." In appropriating this power, we can ask God for things and get them.

What is the dynamic principle Jesus shared with His disciples? It has, first of all, to do with *faith.* But it is not merely any kind of faith. Nor is it the world's ordinary view of faith. It is more than a strong belief. It is the "God kind of faith." It is a specific kind of faith originating with God and shared by us, a faith power in which we can become partners. It is a positive condition in which we partake of the power and reality of God by believing His Word (see Matthew 17:20).

Peter tells us that by appropriating the promises of God we become "partakers of the divine nature," or in other words we share in the very nature of God (II Peter 1:4). Whatever kind of belief God has, we share in. And, of course, God's beliefs are anchored to the absolute truth and reality of things as they really are. It might seem strange for us to use the word "believe" in connection with God, but that is only because we are accustomed to attaching some form of doubt to the word. If we are not quite sure, we say, "I *believe* so." But God is absolutely sure of all things. In fact, all things are there because He commanded them to be there. When we share in God's nature, then, we develop a faith that is absolute in its certainty, with no shade of doubting.

Jesus is saying that if we can have that same kind of certainty about God, His promises and His power, our words can take on new power and we can "have what we say." To show how powerful this principle is, Jesus Himself used the example of moving a mountain! And Jesus was not given to exaggeration.

YOU HAVE WHAT YOU SAY

Now let's see how this idea works in life. To a lesser degree, it is a principle working in the natural world as well as the supernatural. There is a sense in which we all "have what we say." We get things by using some form of verbal communication, whether written or spoken. An alcoholic "has what he says" because he has ordered the drinks that have ruined his life. A man who has stood before a marriage altar and said, "I do," has what he has said! Those two little words have changed many of our lives to a considerable degree, it must be admitted!

But in our relationship with God this takes on new meaning, because God is telling us we can tap the great reserves of His power to bring things to pass by the spoken word. And this is not just a principle reserved for the apostles. In the book of James we read: "The effectual fervent prayer of a righteous man availeth much. Elias was a man subject to like passions as we are, and he prayed earnestly that it might not rain: and it rained not on the earth by the space of three years and six months" (James 5:16,17). In the preceding verses James was admonishing his readers to pray for sick people to get well and for sinners to have their sins forgiven. Then he uses the example of a man like us, with the same problems, who stopped the rain for three and a half years! Elijah had hurled his words like thunderbolts into the sky and the rain stopped. He loosed them again three and a half years later and the rain resumed!

James uses this remarkable man as an example to teach us how powerful our words can be if we have "the God kind of faith." The "faith chapter" in Hebrews (chapter 11) tells us how faithful people of all ages used their faith for remarkable ends: "Who through faith subdued kingdoms, wrought righteousness, obtained promises, stopped the mouths of lions, Quenched the violence of fire, escaped the edge of the sword, out of weakness were made strong" (Hebrews 11:33,34).

How do we get such power? We must first believe in the absolute reality of a God who is here, now, available, working and all-powerful. Merely a vague idea that there is a God "out there somewhere" won't do it. We have grown up with the idea that if we want something, we go to friends, or our bank accounts or some government agency. God wants us to know we can go directly to Him, ask and receive. He is right there, here and now. We need look no further for a reward than to Him: "But without faith it is impossible to please him: for he that cometh to God must believe that He is, and that He is a rewarder of them that diligently seek him" (Hebrews 11:6).

If we can only settle the fact that God is abundantly available to us, that His power is reserved in our behalf, that His promises are there to claim, we can go into the mountain-moving business.

But most of the mountains that have to be moved are spiritual. The mountain of unbelief, for one. The overwhelming majority of people I talk to will discount the life-changing idea I have been presenting. Don't you wonder why so many refuse to accept God's Word? A man picked up his Bible one time and said, "One of these days someone is going to come along and simply believe this Book. Then we'll all be embarrassed!"

One day I stood with several of the men of our church on a lonely, isolated hill covered with woods. We had no resources but our faith. We said to one another, "Let's build here." We said it, we believed it, and it became a reality. Soon, earth-moving machines began to move tons of earth. Concrete poured into ditches, block was stacked on block as walls began to emerge. Framing members came together as trucks hauled men and materials to the building site. Today, there is a fine 20,000 square-foot plant where a patch of woods once stood. Before we walked out on that hill, nobody ever thought of building a church building there. But we said it, and now "we have what we said!"

As we literally moved a small mountain, replacing it with modern buildings, God was telling us what can be done when godly faith is coupled with the power of words. You can have what you say! With faith in God, you can command certain spiritual energy to literally move mountains.

The reason for so few mountain-movers is that there are so few people who believe that mountains can be moved. There is a pathetic gap between what we say we believe and the kind of belief we practice. If we are willing to believe it, our words can have the remarkable power of those of our spiritual forefathers.

Chapter Five

SAYING THE SAME THING

Not many times, even in the Bible, are we privileged to see anything as imposing and dramatic as the opening scene in the book of Job. After introducing this unusual character, God pulls back the curtain dividing earth and Heaven to let us have a look at an awesome scene. The angels have congregated before Jehovah, and with them is the accuser, the arch enemy of all believers of all ages—Satan. There is a struggle, a conflict. The stakes are high, and the battlefield is the mind of a man!

God throws out the challenge. He has a man who is unique, spiritually powerful and undefiled in his lineage. Furthermore, he has such faith that even his great riches are not able to make him self-dependent. He takes his case to Heaven regularly, building a fortress of prayer to keep his children from presuming upon God. So strong is his trust, God has built a bulwark around him so that the accuser has been unable to penetrate with his fiery arrows.

In fact, this is the point of Satan's attack. We can almost hear him snarling as he insinuates, "Doth Job fear God for nought? Hast not thou made an hedge about him, and about his house, and about all that he hath on every side? thou hast blessed the work of his hands, and his substance is increased in the land. But put forth thine hand now, and touch all that he hath, and he will curse thee to thy face" (Job 1:9-11).

Satan charged that the only reason Job revered God was for His blessings. If only the blessings were withheld, Satan reasoned, Job would not fear God, he would curse Him, turning on his former Benefactor. On what did this whole test pivot? Upon what Job would say!

In other passages in the book we see this borne out: "Then Job arose, and rent his mantle, and shaved his head, and fell down upon the ground, and worshipped. And said" (Job 1:20,21). "Then said his wife unto him, Dost thou still retain thine integrity? curse God and die" (Job 2:9). "In all this did not Job sin with his lips" (Job 2:10). "Then Job answered and said . . . Shall vain words have an end? . . . I also could speak as ye do: if your soul were in my soul's stead, I could heap up words against you . . . But I would strengthen you with my mouth" (Job 16:1-5). "Oh that my words were now written! oh that they were printed in a book! That they were graven with an iron pen and lead in the rock for ever! For I know that my redeemer liveth" (Job 19:23-25). "The Lord said to Eliphaz the Temanite, My wrath is kindled against thee, and against thy two friends: for ye have not spoken of me the thing that is right, as my servant Job hath" (Job 42:7).

While angels looked on, the activity around the throne of Heaven was poised in its infinite attention to what a man on earth would say! His words did not die out when the sound waves played out their course, but travelled a spiritual wave length beyond the stars, playing a superbly important role in the spiritual conflict raging in the heavens.

"SAYING WITH" GOD

There are two distinct messages travelling the spiritual circuits of the universe. One of them comes from God, the Source of all truth. God cannot be distinguished from the truth in any way. That is, there is nothing that can be called the truth if it does not coincide with what God says. A person can take a number of facts and come to a faulty conclusion, as the evolutionist does, and not be speaking the truth. Stringing a few facts together does not make truth unless it leads to God and what He says. God is truth. We cannot say accurately, "Since God cannot lie, He must be telling the truth." It is more accurate to say, "It is true because God said it." Whatever God says is true.

The other message is the lie. It started in Eden as soon as Satan asked, "Yea, hath God said?" (Genesis 3:1). Satan is not beyond quoting Scripture for his purposes, but he always comes to a faulty conclusion. When he tempted the Son of God, he quoted Scripture to Him (Matthew 4). Satan wants to cause us to come to a wrong conclusion about the meaning of life, about things as they really are, and about God, even twisting the Scripture to prove a point. Had Job cursed God, his conclusion would have been faulty because he would have discounted all God's past goodness and focused only on the present difficulty: "But he said unto [his wife], Thou speakest as one of the foolish women speaketh. What? shall we receive good at the hand of God, and shall we not receive evil? In all this did not Job sin with his lips" (Job 2:10).

Satan's intention was that Job would curse God. One of the meanings of "curse" is to "pray against" or "speak against." What we have in view here is a kind of speech that is not merely harmless, as most people imagine. It is a spiritual action of the most serious consequences.

And it does not have to involve profanity, as we often imagine. We could be guilty of this sin each time we utter any bitterness or complaint in a time of testing.

The opposite of "curse' is the word, "confess." It means to "speak the same" or "say with." The idea involved is to align our words with the real, God-centered view of the world. Whatever the world is, as God has made it and maintains it; whatever God designed our lives to be, in spite of testings and trials, we "say with" God. Our words line up with His truth.

THE MIND OF GOD

The correct, God-oriented view of the world is the one we find in His Word, which is His revealed mind. In His Word, He opens His mind to us and shows us what the world is really like. We are besieged by all kinds of "experts" who want to tell us what the world is really like. The philosopher-scientist tells us it is a merely chemical or material world. The doctor tells us that health is the vital thing. The journalist wants us to know all the sensational things that are happening, thinking awareness of events is the major thing. To the athlete, it is a world of sports. To the entertainer, all the world is, as Shakespeare said, a stage. The military man majors on his arsenal. How confused we would be if we got our "world view" from all these people. We would have to change it every hour!

To come to a knowledge of reality, or truth, we have to share God's view of the world. In fact, the Scriptural version of wisdom is "seeing the world from God's point of view." To confess is to share that point of view with others by what we say, to "say the same" as God. One of the first viewpoints we have to accept from God is the fact that we are sinful, thus confessing our sin, or saying the same thing about it that He does (I John 1:9).

THE NEW TESTAMENT SPEAKS

What does the New Testament have to say about this principle? If the Old Testament patriarch, Job, could reach Heaven with his words and be the focal point of a tumultuous conflict in Heaven, does the same thing happen to us?

Jesus had something pointed to say about this. In Matthew 10:32,33 He lays down a mighty principle for living: "Whosoever therefore shall confess me before men, him will I confess also before my Father which is in heaven. But whosoever shall deny me before men, him will I also deny before my Father which is in heaven."

A "therefore" is an arrow pointing back to something said earlier. What does the "therefore" in Matthew 10 point to? Jesus had sent His disciples out to preach in the towns and villages of Israel. In verse 14 He said, "And whosoever shall not receive you, nor hear your words, when ye depart out of that house or city, shake off the dust of your feet." In verses 26,27 after warning them of how they would be persecuted for their words, Jesus admonishes: "Fear them not therefore: for there is nothing covered, that shall not be revealed; and hid, that shall not be known. What I tell you in darkness, that speak ye in light: and what ye hear in the ear, that preach ye upon the housetops." He was talking about the words they spoke in the presence of others.

Usually when we think of His saying "confess me before men," we think of the point at which a man makes his confession of faith in Christ. But this principle is much deeper than that. This has to do with His disciples *confessing that Jesus Christ was Lord* in the face of unrelenting persecution. They later knew full well what He meant, for almost all of them were martyred for confessing the lordship of Jesus Christ before the world. No wonder the world didn't like it. The word "Lord" means ruler, boss, absolute sovereign. They were putting Christ over everybody else and everything else in the world. The reaction of the world was, "We will not have this man to rule over us."

Jesus was laying down a principle for our total life experience as it is related to what we say. As we view the scene in the book of Job, we learn that Heaven is vitally concerned over whether we will "speak against" or "speak with" God. And Jesus said if we deny Him in any given circumstances we lose power before the throne: "But whosoever shall deny me before men, him will I also deny before my Father which is in heaven" (Matthew 10:33).

The two spiritual messages, truth and error, are vividly contrasted in every area of our lives. One of the most consistent lies of Satan is that God is not good. His whole appeal to Eve began with the idea that God was withholding something from them. He still preaches that false message. We frequently hear the argument, "If there is a God, why does He allow such-and-such to happen?" "Why did that little baby die?"

Somehow people have grown to think that instead of being grateful to God for His blessings, for life and beauty and health and a host of other things, Christians take them for granted and want only to blame God for the things we consider bad or unfair. Satan was careful not to remind Eve of all the trees of which they could eat, but only accused God of being unfair because of the one tree that was forbidden.

It is in this area that the confession of the Christian touches a tender spot. Our message is that God is good! He loved us, sought us, and sent His Son to die for us.

We live in the spirit of John 3:16. What happens, then, when a professing Christian gets into trouble and murmurs, gripes and complains? The message that comes through to the world is that God is *not* good. Translated, a bitter complaining spirit means: "If God really loved me, He wouldn't let this happen to me."

That was Satan's hope in the case of Job. But Job surprised him. Bereft of his material possessions, left without his work force and even robbed of his children, his most precious possession, Job did not speak against God. Instead, he fell on the ground and worshiped! "Naked came I out of my mother's womb, and naked shall I return thither" (Job 1:21). In other words, "I didn't have anything when I started, and all I got came from the Lord. If He wants to take away what He gives me, it doesn't change God in the least. He's still good."

Since we can trust the Scriptural record, we realize that there are two who have access to a heavenly audience. One is Christ, our Advocate, who stands before the Father to plead our case. The other is Satan, who stands to accuse. The basis upon which they deal with us has a great deal to do with the kind of confession we send up. A bitter word does not give our Advocate anything to "confess before the Father." On the other hand, it does give the accuser, Satan, the ammunition he needs to slander us before the throne.

There is victory, power and blessing in our confession, if it is a good confession. The moment it is registered in Heaven, power radiates from the throne of God to bless us and those around us. The spiritual communication system of this universe radiates the winning news—a confession that is compatible with the truth of God! After all, we do not live for this present world. We already know it is resting under sin and judgment. Our citizenship is in Heaven:

> These all died in faith, not having received the promises, but having seen them afar off, and were persuaded of them, and embraced them, and confessed that they were strangers and pilgrims on the earth.
> ...wherefore God is not ashamed to be called their God: for he hath prepared for them a city.
>
> Hebrews 11:13,16

Chapter Six

IS THERE A RECORD OF OUR WORDS?

At a dramatic moment in his discourse with his three friends, Job rises to a crescendo of exclamation: "Oh that my words were now written! oh that they were printed in a book! That they were graven with an iron pen and lead in the rock forever" (Job 19:23,24). God answered that prayer "exceeding abundantly" (see Ephesians 3:20). He went even further, and permitted it to be recorded in the eternal Word of God, which will endure beyond the time when the stars burn out of their sockets and the mountains have wasted to dust. His words, along with those of his friends, were recorded.

The Apostle James has a comment about the unjust farmers of his day who were cheating their laborers: "Behold, the hire of the labourers who have reaped down your fields, which is of you kept back by fraud, crieth: and the cries of them which have reaped are entered into the ears of the Lord of sabaoth" (James 5:4). The cries of the laborers were on record in Heaven.

When God confronted Cain after Abel had been slain at his hand, He said: "What hast thou done? the voice of thy brother's blood crieth unto me from the ground" (Genesis 4:10). In commenting on this, the writer of Hebrews tells us that Abel, "being dead yet speaketh" (Hebrews 11:4).

Scientists have developed listening devices so sensitive that they can pick up sound vibrations hours after the original sound was made. In these days of sophisticated recording devices it is not hard for us to understand the preservation of a voice. Many churches can now keep their pastor's sermons stacked neatly on shelves to be instantly replayed. Computers store millions of items of not only printed information, but verbal sounds as well. Surely, man is not more advanced than God. If we have developed this technology within the relatively short period of a lifetime, God has not lagged behind.

It is sobering to think that God has on record every word ever spoken or thought! Mercifully, our memories blank out most of what we have said, or what has been said to us. But God's spiritual recording equipment has it all preserved. The things said in secret and in public are all accurately stored away, subject to instant recall.

Jesus put it this way: "O generation of vipers, how can ye, being evil, speak good things? for out of the abundance of the heart the mouth speaketh. A good man out of the good treasure of the heart bringeth forth good things; and an evil man out of the evil treasure bringeth forth evil things. But I say unto you, That every idle word that men shall speak, they shall give account thereof in the day of judgment" (Matthew 12:34-36). By "idle word," we assume Jesus meant any word that did not profit others or bring glory to God in some way. Just think of the multitude of foolish, slanderous and profane speech men will cringe about in the day of judgment!

It is even more sobering to realize that there is a record of the words of others whose speech we should have heeded. For instance, Proverbs tells us: "Whoso stoppeth his ears at the cry of the poor, he also shall cry himself, but shall not be heard" (Proverbs 21:13). As the cry of innocent blood comes forth from the ground and the cry of the defrauded laborers ascends to Heaven, the cry of the poor, gone unheeded, stands as a record against those who stop their ears at its cry! And what of those who hear the gospel and ignore it? It will ring in their ears for all eternity.

YEA AND NAY

In knowing that Heaven is recording our words, there are a number of precautions we may well take. One of them is to regard the *volume* of our words—how much we say. In the Sermon on the Mount, Jesus warned against improper oaths, adding that our communication should be kept to a minimum (Matthew 5:37). James observes that piety with an unbridled tongue is empty (James 1:26). The Psalmist, aware of the dangers of overtalking, prayed, "Set a watch, O Lord, before my mouth; keep the door of my lips" (Psalm 141:3). And again, "Let the words of my mouth, and the meditation of my heart, be acceptable in thy sight, O Lord, my strength, and my redeemer" (Psalm 19:14).

We all know people who just can't be quiet. In gentler days such a person was called a "boor" because his inappropriate speech marked him as ill-mannered and awkward. Perhaps we live in such a clamorous age nowadays that such behavior is more acceptable. The Scriptures teach that our abundance of ill-founded words reveals a number of things about us. Our words are tattletales, spreading the true condition of our hearts out before others as if they turned us inside out! It is a pity we do not hear our words as others hear them.

Voluminous verbiage reveals a spirit that is unteachable (Proverbs 29:11; James 1:18-21). One of the marks of a wise man is that he reserves comment until he is sure of the wisdom of what he says. I write this with a red face as I remember how I spent my first few months in college trying to "straighten out" the teachers! Nothing betrays a lack of knowledge quite so much as an unhinged tongue.

The wise man is a listener. He displays a learner's spirit. He realizes that one must first learn before he can teach. Indeed, most men of wisdom have to be prodded into giving their counsel, so reluctant are they to give out information that might be incorrect. The wisest of them all, Solomon, observed this: "Counsel in the heart of man is like deep water; but a man of understanding will draw it out" (Proverbs 20:5). Usually, however, we tend to think *many words* are indicative of *much wisdom.* The Pharisees were not the only ones who thought they would be heard for their much speaking. It is a common ailment. Preachers, for one, need to remember that the longest sermons are not always the best sermons. Think of that masterpiece in John, chapter 3!

SEASONED WITH SALT

In addition to the quantity, when we think of God's heavenly recorder, we need to think of the spiritual *quality* of our words. All our words *do* have a spiritual quality, for words cannot be spiritually neutral.

Two of the Ten Commandments have to do with what we say. Jesus warned us to "swear not at all" (Matthew 5:34). On the positive side, Paul told the Colossians, "Let your speech be always with grace, seasoned with salt, that ye may know how ye ought to answer every man" (Colossians 4:6). Since our words are capable of having eternal spiritual significance, we may well mark each word before we speak.

Through our words we can encourage, rebuke, exhort, witness for Christ, pray, sing, praise, worship, preach, testify, and even vote to support a missionary! We can also slander, sow discord, murmur, curse, and remain silent when we ought to witness. Almost everything to do with our experience in our churches is related to communication. God is constantly monitoring the spiritual quality of our words.

JUSTIFIED AND CONDEMNED

Perhaps as much as anything, our words are being recorded as a matter of justification and condemnation. Jesus said, "For by thy words thou shalt be justified, and by thy words thou shalt be condemned" (Matthew 12:37).

The Bible uses the word "justified" in at

least two senses. One of them is in describing God's judicial action in declaring His people to be righteous before Him (Romans 4:5). The other sense is in how the world is able to measure our faith. In itself, faith is an invisible quality. But God says true, Biblical faith can be measured by what people observe in our lives. James tells us that a person who claims to have faith, but who has no visible, outward indication of that faith, has a dead faith rather than the living, Spirit-borne faith of the saints. In a very striking way, God speaks through James about a hypothetical case. We see a group meeting together who say they have faith (James 2:1-4). Their faith is being shown by their words. A rich man enters the assembly, and the usher steps up to offer him the best seat in the house, saying "unto him, Sit thou here in a good place" (verse 3). But God is listening.

Next, a poor man enters the assembly. He doesn't look as if he can contribute much to this congregation, so the usher says, "stand thou there, or sit here under my footstool" (verse 3). As James continues to develop his somewhat painful argument, he exhorts, "So speak ye, and so do, as they that shall be judged by the law of liberty" (verse 12). God says our faith is not measured so much by what we say on our statement of faith as by what we say to those who enter our assembly.

Going on with his devastating logic,

James asks, "What doth it profit, my brethren, though a man say he hath faith, and have not works? Can [that] faith save him?" (verse 14). Here is a man who says he has faith. He probably has it on a written creed. He no doubt stands and gives testimony that he has faith. His name is, no doubt, on the roll of the church, so he has expressed some degree of faith in order to be a member of the assembly. But that is not what God is listening to. God is recording his words spoken to a hungry brother:

"If a brother or sister be naked, and destitute of daily food, And one of you say unto them, Depart in peace, be ye warmed and filled; notwithstanding ye give them not those things which are needful to the body; what doth it profit?" (verses 15,16). This man's claim for faith is unjustified because his empty words betray it for what it is, a dead faith. When he opens his mouth, only dead things come out! Perhaps that is what Paul had in mind when he quoted: "Their throat is an open sepulchre" (Romans 3:13). The man in question in James' example has a confession of faith, but it is empty, dead and false. His words betray it for what it is.

It is in this sense that Jesus said we will be justified or condemned by our words. A man can go along through life, congratulating himself on his religion, all the time deluding himself into thinking he is a man of faith. But all his words are "on tape."

God is recording them. When he makes his claim for faith before God's throne, he will cringe in horror as his own words are played back to him!

Our generation has witnessed this in a dramatic and powerful way during the Watergate years. Many claims and counter claims were made, but the final outcome of the case was decided by the words that had been recorded in the Oval Office and other White House chambers. The testimony of the words was the "smoking gun" that established the blame for the cover-up alleged by the prosecution. In the end, their words did them in. The evidence could not be denied.

James is not saying, any more than Jesus, that it is our words that provide the merit for our justification. That is reckoned on the work of Jesus Christ on the cross. But our words are a barometer of the true condition of our hearts.

A group of friendly people gather to chat, only to learn later that their host has hidden a small cassette recorder that has caught the entire conversation. How surprised the guests are to hear how silly they sound! One person cries out, "That doesn't sound like me!" How differently our words sound when they are going into our ears, rather than coming out of our mouths. But from the Scriptures we learn that *every word* is permanent, eternal, inscribed in Heaven. Somebody's listening!

Chapter Seven

WORDS WITH HOOKS

One of the things said of the serpent employed by Satan in the garden of Eden was that he was beautiful. To be more specific, the divine record says he was *subtle*. One meaning given for this word is "delicately skillful." We can be sure temptations will not usually come our way in work clothes. They will most likely come clothed in the more comely attire of silk and purple. If that is true, we can be sure that the most tempting words are those clothed in the most beauty.

Sometimes a salesman, either in the flesh or the bright light of our TV set, will sell us the things we do not need with the art of clever, contrived speech. He will try his best to charm us into thinking we really need things we do not need.

An anti-Christian university professor will spin his yarn of atheistic humanism into a dissertation of axioms and long words. Actually, he may be hiding a lot of ignorance with his "educationese."

The false theologian who does not believe the Bible to be God's authoritative Word will nevertheless use the Bible to prove his point. He will hide his message of falsehood and deception behind beautiful poetry, appealing philosophy and theological words. But when we strip away the subtle beauty of his words, it is still the same old lie.

Most of us realize Satan will tempt with perfume and silk, chrome and paint, flash and glitter, but few of us seem to realize how craftily he can use the beauty of *words*. The subject bears some investigation.

KNOWLEDGE: SHOULD WE GET ALL WE CAN?

A popular notion nowadays is that we ought to take everything in, get all the knowledge we can. "College is man's best friend," we hear. Certain novelists assure us that pornography presents life as it really is, and that we are not complete until we know these things. And so school libraries include what was once considered pornography.

We have been told in the last couple of years that if we can just get enough of our young people into the college classroom we will enter utopia. One of the things we have forgotten is that the first limitation put upon man was a limitation of *knowledge!* It was the Tree of Knowledge of Good and Evil that our first parents were forbidden to eat of. And, remember, the temptation to ignore this command came in a very pleasant and beautiful form (Genesis 3:6).

Paul indirectly warns us about the effects of "excellency of speech or of wisdom" and "enticing words of man's wisdom" in the "wisdom" chapter of I Corinthians—chapter 2. Some of the things he warns us about are:

"That your faith should not stand in the wisdom of men, but in the power of God" (verse 5).

"Yet not the wisdom of this world, nor of the princes of this world, that come to naught" (verse 6).

"Which none of the princes of this world knew" (verse 8).

"Not in the words which man's wisdom teacheth, but which the Holy Ghost teacheth; comparing spiritual things with spiritual" (verse 13).

"But the natural man receiveth not the things of the Spirit of God" (verse 14).

Who belongs in the category of "the princes of this world" and the "natural man" as not being able to compare spiritual things with spiritual? Can we consider the entertainer, the poet, the unconverted scientist, the novelist, the rock musician, the politician, the "secular" teacher, in addition to the one who promotes a false religious cult? How can we spot the person who would beguile us with "enticing words of man's wisdom"? How can we learn to avoid the beautiful, baited word that can hook our minds to a false idea? How can we limit our knowledge to what God wants us to know?

HOW TO SPOT
SPIRITUAL KNOWLEDGE

We know that our world contains hidden spiritual truths not evident to the uninitiated eye. There is a whole world of spiritual dynamics out there that the mind of a "natural man" is closed to. He cannot know them, not even if he is educated and gifted. No matter how clever his words, he is always starting from a false and devastating idea of life. Paul tells us this is the starting point. He tells us what the one central idea of all life and wisdom is: "For I determined not to know any thing among you, save Jesus Christ, and him crucified" (I Corinthians 2:2).

From this we can learn that any situation, any learning experience that would not admit this idea is false, unrealistic, and to be avoided. We somehow have gained the idea that this central issue, man's need for redemption and what God did to meet it, is a "religious idea" that we discuss only in church or with religious people. To all the other fields of knowledge—math, history, science, the humanities, language—we have unwisely given the label, "secular." One of the root meanings of the word *secular* is "belonging to an age." It is talking about this world, or "age," as compared to the dynamic world of reality described in the Bible. Paul had a grasp of the idea of the word when he spoke of "the princes of this world" (I Corinthians 2:6). Many of us in this age, unfortunately, have put most of our quest for knowledge into the pretty basket of "this world" and reserved only a tiny little bit for our Sunday morning worship service. Paul informs us that this is a completely unrealistic view of things as they really are. We have to *start* with the message of the cross in order to be on target with our knowledge.

THE ATTITUDE OF WORDS

The second characteristic of true wisdom, the message mighty in Spirit, is its attitude. It is humility: "And I was with you in weakness, and in fear, and in much trembling" (I Corinthians 2:3). John the Baptist was a man mighty in the Spirit. When he was asked who he was, he spoke of his own unworthiness and pointed to the Lamb of God! The great prophets were men of few and simple words, and Jesus Himself spoke in such a way that "the common people heard him gladly." No room for the haughty, arrogant spirit of the "supermind" here!

The man who speaks in the might of the Spirit rather than man's wisdom realizes a grave responsibility. He knows anyone who "messes around with a man's mind" has entered a sacred sanctuary and will be accordingly held responsible by the one who created that mind (James 3:1). No wonder Paul trembled! (I Corinthians 2:3).

SIMPLE WORDS

A third characteristic of the message mighty in Spirit has to do with the words themselves. Paul said he did not come with "enticing" or "persuasable" words (I Corinthians 2:4). It is characteristic of the person who is speaking with spiritual power that he does not depend upon the cleverness or the persuasiveness of his vocabulary to convince his hearers, but upon a much greater power—the energy of the Spirit of God. Words are often missiles of Satan's power, too. If he has not changed his methods, we can be sure that beauty and attractiveness are the powers he uses. But the Spirit-led speaker does not depend upon that. This is not to say that a spiritual, godly teacher cannot be correct in his diction and be in command of a good vocabulary. But the power does not lie in the choice of words, but in how they are used by the Holy Spirit. We should observe whether a man's words reflect the love of God, which is a fruit of the Spirit. If they do not, no matter how clever, they are "as sounding brass, or a tinkling cymbal" (I Corinthians 13:1).

WHAT'S HIS MOTIVE?

A fourth characteristic of godly, Spirit-led speech has to do with what the speaker is trying to accomplish. What is his goal? Self-gain? To cast a doubt on the truth? His motive will usually come through. Paul stated the goal of his speech this way: "That your faith should not stand in the wisdom of men, but in the power of God" (I Corinthians 2:5). There was no self-gain in view here. Paul, the Apostle, a man of mighty intellect, deliberately subjected that intellect to simplicity of speech so his hearers would not concentrate on the messenger, but upon the message and the One who commissioned him to preach it. The Spirit-led speaker never calls attention to himself.

What about our conversation in the ordinary channels of life? Can these things apply? Can our talk in the shop, the market and at parties reflect the cross of Christ, spiritual power and reality, without seeming artificial or affected? Yes. If a man's philosophy of life is right, it will come out in every word he says. If he is led by the Spirit, he doesn't have to use theological terminology to impress people. They will know they are listening to a spiritual man. In fact, a strained "religious" type of talk is the very thing Paul warned against.

God's purpose is that we do not live in two different worlds, a secular one and a sacred one. "Glory" and "hallelujah" are nice words, but one does not have to use them to be spiritual. Our knowledge of Him should be so persuasive we will reflect His truth in all our conversation as naturally as we breathe.

EVERYBODY LOVES A MYSTERY

Jesus spoke in parables, hiding His deep truths from the careless ears of His profane hearers, carefully avoiding "casting His pearls before swine." God has locked His truth into His creation, and Jesus used creation to teach the mysteries of the kingdom of God. Every tree, rock, brook and animal say something of Him if we care to listen. The reason Jesus spoke with such power was that He turned the whole world into a sermon.

The trouble is, the "secular" mind is so completely void of understanding that it cannot hear the sermon. It is hidden from view, Paul said, "But we speak the wisdom of God in a mystery" (I Corinthians 2:7). A mystery is something hidden from some and revealed to others. Satan convinced Eve that there was something "out there" she needed to learn—something that God had unlovingly withheld from her. She learned, too late, that all she needed to know was to be gained through simple communication with God!

We haven't changed much. We are led by fancy, high-sounding words down all kinds of trails to space ships and spare parts, amoeba and genes, witches and demons, stars and superstars, success formulas and bright new, yet dismally tragic, utopias. But all the while, the real mystery is God. Who can fathom His truth and explore His riches?

"O the depth of the riches both of the wisdom and knowledge of God! how unsearchable are his judgments, and his ways past finding out!" (Romans 11:33). If we were to fly to every star, uncover every rock, and search all the ocean's depths, we could still not exhaust the full mystery of Him and His plan for us! Every legitimate field of knowledge cries to understand and appropriate His wisdom. And all the search for true wisdom ends with Him. Other things may contain some truth, but it is not *the* truth.

The only reason Satan leads us down "rabbit trails" is to turn us from the pursuit of knowledge about God. The more we know about Him, the more we will come to the One of whom it is said, "In whom are hid all the treasures of wisdom and knowledge" (Colossians 2:3).

Words, words, words. We hear so many

of them. We grow weary of them. But when all the sound and fury are gone, only the ones that speak of Him will count. And God warns us to stay away from any intellectual path and disregard any words, no matter how beautiful, that cannot lead us to the knowledge of Christ. The very power of lying words is in their beauty and attractiveness, cleverly designed to lead us to the wrong destination.

Chapter Eight

THUNDERBOLTS
TO HEAVEN

The Old Testament saint, Jabez, loosed a thunderbolt to Heaven and God stopped what He was doing to note the event and record it for posterity and eternity. Surely there were other people in those days going about the *motions* of prayer, but this man really prayed.

A popular notion abroad today is that prayer does not affect God in any way, but changes only those who pray. The Scriptures teach differently. God heard the prayers of Solomon (II Chronicles 7:12), Abraham (Genesis 20:17), Moses (Numbers 11:2), Hannah (I Samuel 1:27), Samuel (I Samuel 8:6,7), Elijah (James 5:17), Elisha (II Kings 6:17,18), Hezekiah (II Kings 19:20), Jonah (Jonah 2:1,10), and many others. For God to "hear" means for Him to acknowledge our prayer. The Scriptures teach that our very words can ascend to Heaven, touch the heart of God and bring results!

One of the most touching scenes in the Bible is found in Revelation 8:1-5. Activity in Heaven is stopped. There is silence. The angels stand in awe. In the presence of God, the prayers of the saints ascend up before the throne and mingle with the incense, a sweet savor before God and His angels. So remarkable is the idea that men can talk to Heaven, God gives it a prominent place throughout His Word. He interrupts the chronicles of Israel to mention the remarkable prayer of Jabez, and when Ananias is sent to baptize Paul, the Bible points out, "Arise, and go into the street which is called Straight, and enquire in the house of Judas for one called Saul, of Tarsus: for behold, he prayeth (Acts 9:11).

A PREMIUM ACTIVITY

Prayer is such an important activity in the eyes of God that He says we should carry it on unceasingly (I Thessalonians 5:17), tenaciously (Luke 18:1-8), intensely (Matthew 7:7-11) and with importunity (Luke 11:5-8). The various elements of prayer, such as adoration, confession, supplication, intercession and thanksgiving are well known to most of us. Not so well known, however, is the premium God puts upon the words themselves. It is not the extent of our vocabulary or the beauty of our phrases that impresses Him (Matthew 6:7). But though our words be halting and meager, we can be sure He ascribes power to our words, which are the vehicles of our thoughts.

It is here that many of us fail. We feel that if we cannot say things right before a crowd, we will surely have trouble coming up with any words to utter in the presence of God. But *one word* can have great power. When Peter was sinking in the water, he cried out, "Lord, save me" (Matthew 15:30). He not only holds the world's record for a mortal walking on water, but he probably also uttered the world's shortest prayer. And it worked!

When the disciples asked the Lord to teach them to pray, He shared with them the prayer that has been uttered millions of times around the world, yet it contains only 66 words. (Our modern bureaucrats and theologians would have stretched it to 66 pages!) There's no reason to be reluctant to pray because we cannot think of eloquent words, or even enough words. Our words, though humble and few, have power at the throne of God (Romans 8:26).

Jesus offered His remarkable prayer of intercession (John 17) while walking over the Kidron Valley. Before that He told the disciples their words could plug them into Heaven's power: "If ye abide in me, and my words abide in you, ye shall ask what ye will, and it shall be done unto you"

(John 15:7). While our heart attitude and relationship to God are vital to prayer, they do not alone make up the prayers we are to make to God. If there were no *communication,* if we could not actually express what we want to in *language,* prayer would be meaningless. As in any other form of conversation, there must be an exchange of words, if only thought silently in our minds.

When Samuel F.B. Morse was to send a message over a test telegraph wire from Washington, D.C. to Baltimore, he tapped out "What hath God wrought?" What a wonder that wires could carry words from one city to another! And what a wonder that our words, coming from our own hearts, can travel all the way to God and express our desires and needs to Him! Prayed from a true heart, every faltering word contains great power. We have an audience day and night with the ultimate Power in the universe, the living God!

A STRONG FORTRESS

Not only do we learn that our words have the power to move Heaven, but they can also build an impenetrable fortress around our thought life. We are given this insight in Philippians 4:6,7: "Be careful for nothing; but in every thing by prayer and supplication with thanksgiving let your requests be made known unto God. And the peace of God, which passeth all understanding, shall keep your hearts and minds through Christ Jesus."

By substituting prayer for worry, the Bible says we can have a peace so strong it is impossible to understand. And we do not even have the responsibility of "keeping the peace." We build the prayer, but God builds the wall. The verse declares, "The peace of God ... shall keep (garrison, or guard) your hearts and minds." Our words of prayer and thanksgiving pull down the battlements of Heaven around our minds. Who can penetrate "the peace of God" with even the strongest of weapons? And the Peace Officer who keeps the peace is the strong One Himself, Jesus Christ! The text tells us that peace "shall keep your hearts and minds through Christ Jesus."

So powerful are our words of "prayer and supplication with thanksgiving" that the enemy cannot enter with his conflict and unrest. Like some kind of force field, our words keep him out because they command the power of One who is greater.

Satan works through our words. If only we could get hold of this, our lives would be drastically changed. It is during moments of conflict and unrest that we suffer our greatest spiritual harm. Caught off guard, we lash out at others, starting things into motion that spoil our peace and embroil us in conflict. This only leads to more serious damage as the one against whom we rail is also unsettled, retaliating in kind. All conflict arises this way. The only cure is the peace of God.

After telling us how to maintain an orderly relationship with others (I Peter 2:11-21), Peter gives us a glimpse into the prayer life of our Lord: "Who, when he was reviled, reviled not again; when he suffered, he threatened not; but committed himself to him that judgeth righteously" (verse 23). What calmness and perfect peace our Lord displayed as He stood before Pilate. With what regal bearing He stood—a Rock in a storm! But the key is found in the fact that He "railed not again" but rather "committed himself to him that judgeth righteously." The same peace is available to us. Satan trembles and retreats when men pray!

THE POWER OF
APPROPRIATE WORDS

Big Jim was the beer-drinking buddy of Sam Sloan before Sam was converted. When Jim's car went off the road at high speed, crashing into a sign, the authorities concluded that Jim's heavy drinking had caused the accident. Sam visited Jim in the hospital, urging him to just "trust the Lord." Sam had prayed with him.

After his recovery from his injuries, Jim went back to his old ways. But he would occasionally tell the fellows in a bar that he knew "the man upstairs" had helped him get over his injuries. What did Jim's choice of words reveal about his opinion of God? How important are the appropriate words when we pray?

Although we can be sure the "Spirit helpeth our infirmities" when we cannot frame the proper words in our prayer, it is also evident that in teaching us to pray, God is also teaching us something about the proper way to address Deity, the proper attitude to have toward an omnipotent Authority and many other spiritual truths. When the Lord was teaching His disciples to pray, He first cautioned them to pray in secret (Matthew 6:5,6). This was a warning to avoid the kind of display that would tempt them to use empty words. He followed that by warning them against "vain repetitions," or hypocritical, high-sounding words. He then uttered the Model Prayer, an astonishing petition with equally astonishing clarity and brevity.

Every word in that prayer is significant. For one thing, it teaches us whom to address when we pray: "Our Father." When I was a young man, the best way to get some unwanted lumps was to address my father as "Old Man!" How much more necessary it is to address the God of all creation with the proper term. The Scripture teaches us to make our prayer *to the Father* (Matthew 6:9), *in the Name of the Son* (John 16:23) and *through the Spirit* (Romans 8:26).

This not only teaches us the various

ministries of the Persons of the blessed Godhead, but also gives some important lessons about the gospel. It teaches us, for one thing, that the Father sent the Son, then the Son sent the Spirit after His ascension. It also teaches us that the Son is at the right hand of the Father, interceding for us—thus we pray in the name, or stead, of our divine Intercessor.

We are taught, moreover, to recognize that God is above us, not our equal—"which art in heaven" (Matthew 6:9). The Bible teaches us that God is "high and lifted up" (Isaiah 6:1), and that He "inhabiteth eternity" (57:15). Although we are indwelled by the Holy Spirit, we are not taught to pray to a God who is *within* us, but rather to pray to One who is *above* us.

Jesus' model prayer teaches us the esteem with which we should regard the name of God: "Hallowed be thy name" (Matthew 6:9). It is not at all funny or pleasing to God when men kick His holy name around or hold it in light esteem (Exodus 20:7).

The model prayer further teaches us of His coming kingdom: "Thy kingdom come" (Matthew 6:10). We learn that He will someday descend to this earth, and will put an end to rebellion: "Thy will be done in earth, as it is in heaven" (Matthew 6:10).

This prayer teaches us to be content with His daily provision: "Give us this day our daily bread" (verse 11). It also shows that our relationship with those around us reveals something about our relationship with Him: "And forgive us our debts, as we forgive our debtors" (verse 12). We learn that the thing to fear most is not being unpopular or poor, but being tempted to do evil: "And lead us not into temptation, but deliver us from evil" (verse 13). We learn further that our ultimate responsibility is not to ourselves, but to the God of glory: "For this is the kingdom, and the power, and the glory, for ever, Amen (verse 13).

God is trying to teach us the holiest exercise our lips can participate in—talking to Him. When we learn well, using words that are appropriate and pleasing to Him, great honor is possible for Him and great power for us. We can be sure Satan, the accuser, hates for us to use the words that give God his rightful glory, hence the unprecedented attempt in our day to degrade God with improper language.

The proper words, however, words conceived and taught by God, connect us with the ultimate and available energy that is radiating from His throne. We have only to think of our government officials. Because of the importance and potential of a high office, protocol does not permit one to go ambling into officials' offices throwing out greetings like, "Hi, ol' Buddy!" That is hardly appropriate. Nor will it obtain much favor from the government. God is a much higher authority. While we have been made "nigh by the blood of Christ" (Ephesians 2:13), we do not profane the holy One who inhabits the throne of Heaven.

When we pray right, with the right heart attitude, the appropriate words, and true faith in God, there is no limit to what God can do. Words spoken from a true heart in prayer are thunderbolts that reach to where the power is, the throne of an omnipotent God. Our words have power with God.

Chapter 9

BUILDING WALLS
WITH WORDS

Susan Carrol did not believe in divorce. Brought up in a Christian home, she had been taught that divorce was against everything the Bible taught about marriage. For many years, she had endured suffering at the hand of her husband, while patiently living for Christ. But now, so many unkind things had been said between them it seemed as if reconciliation were impossible. There had been too many cutting words, traumatic arguments and broken promises.

One of the things which made Susan so sad was the number of times she had lost her temper and said things she shouldn't have said. Now, each time she tried to "patch up" their difficulties, her husband would remind her of some things she had said in the past. Stung by guilt and regret, she would try to defend her words, but the emotional situation was so shaky that a new, explosive argument would follow. It seemed hopeless. She reminded him of things he had said in the past, too, and it became a barrage of charges and counter charges, providing more ammunition for future arguments. Finally, she had to admit, the arguments had driven him away. A wall of words had been built that seemed impossible to surmount, and the marriage was tragically broken.

BLESSING FOR CURSING

In the Sermon on the Mount, Jesus cautioned His disciples: "Bless them that curse you" (Matthew 5:44). This seems like such a strange command. What is behind it?

To bless means to say something. We ordinarily think of a "blessing" as some material benefit coming to us as a result of someone's generosity, but the thought in the word has to do with speech. When we "bless" God, as the psalmist did, we say something that ascribes worth to Him. "Curse" also, as we have seen, has to do with speech. In this part of the passage, Jesus was talking about blessing a person who is at odds with us.

Verse 45 reminds us that this makes us like God, "for he maketh his sun to rise on the evil and on the good, and sendeth rain on the just and on the unjust." If we are to be the "children of God," or "in the image of God," we will also bless both the evil and the good. Not that we should approve of the ways of the evil, but we should not return cursing to them.

AMBASSADORS

Let me suggest one possible reason Jesus may have warned His disciples against replying in kind to those who "curse" us. Since we are on a mission, Jesus wants us to leave openings to fulfill our mission of being ambassadors for Him: "Now then we are ambassadors for Christ, as though God did beseech you by us: we pray you in Christ's stead, be ye reconciled to God" (II Corinthians 5:20). The Bible tells us that this changes our whole outlook toward others. A few verses earlier, Paul declared, "If any man be in Christ, he is a new creature" (verse 17).

Before we became ambassadors, we looked at men "after the flesh" (verse 16), and it was natural to reply in kind to those who curse us. But now, we put that behind us, for "old things are passed away" (verse 17). Being an ambassador puts us in a new position altogether. We are no longer representing our own interests, but His interests. He came to reconcile the world; now He is in us reconciling the world to Himself. We are on a special mission for Him.

One of the functions of an ambassador is

to keep the lines of communication open so two alien powers can cooperate. That is called *diplomacy*. Sadly, however, many Christians have shut the door of communications, sealing off any chance to communicate the gospel of Christ to those around them. They have done this by saying unkind things. If blessing had been used instead of cursing the lines of communication would still be open. They have built a steel curtain with their words.

KEEPING THE DOORS OPEN

We are wise to keep the lines of communication open in several different areas of our lives. One of them is in the church: "Rebuke not an elder, but intreat him as a father; and [entreat] the younger men as brethren; [entreat] The elder women as mothers; [entreat] the younger as sisters, with all purity" (I Timothy 5:1,2).

In telling Timothy about how we ought to "behave . . . in the house of God" (I Timothy 3:15), Paul was making the point that we ought to entreat rather than rebuke. This involves a choice of words. The wrong kind of words builds walls that split churches and causes offenses. If a verbal wall is erected between members of the same assembly, it forces the other members to choose which side of the wall they will stand on.

This is so important in New Testament teaching that it is dealt with frequently.

In the job and the market place, the home and the government we are told to stay away from barriers that will hinder our ability to represent the interests of Christ. In the book of I Peter, the apostle tells us how we ought to behave toward a cantankerous employer (I Peter 2:18,19). The passage is well worth studying, especially verses 20-23, in which the suffering Saviour is given as our example, for He "reviled not again" (verse 23). The world knows what Christ is like. And they know we are not good ambassadors if we do not display the same spirit He did. If a mean, unreasonable boss makes our life miserable, we need to stop to remember what was done to Jesus. And then we should behave with the spirit He showed us.

On the job and in the church we are to keep the lines open. We represent Him at all cost. Whenever the world sees Christians stop living for themselves, and start living for the One whom they say they represent, the world will see Him in us! But that is not the most difficult area. The hardest place to live like Jesus is at home. All the pretenses are dropped at home, and our family members see us just as we are.

What about the woman who is living with an unconverted husband? It is hard to be a Christian and meet the demands of one who does not understand or share her beliefs. What is she to do? Thousands of wives have this problem today. Susan Carrol was caught in such a situation. In this passage, the Apostle Peter gives Susan some inspired advice: "Likewise, ye wives, be in subjection to your own husbands; that, if any obey not the word, they also may without the word be won by the conversation of the wives" (I Peter 3:1). Please note that the purpose of all this is to win the husband. The wife is an ambassador for Christ. Now, obviously, if a wife has not caught this vision, or has forgotten it, she is in trouble. If she is representing her own case instead of that of Christ, she is going to fall on hard times.

It is not sex appeal, as some popular writers are suggesting, but a meek and quiet spirit that keeps the lines of communication open so the husband may be won. It is not perfume or lace, but "the ornament of a meek and quiet spirit" (verse 4). Susan Carrol may have realized this too late. She wanted to remain with her husband and try to win him, but it seemed that too many insurmountable walls had been erected by their words.

Is that medicine good only for wives, or does the Bible have something to say on the same subject to the husbands? Let's take a look at verses 7,9: "Likewise, ye husbands; dwell with them according to knowledge, giving honour unto the wife, as unto the weaker vessel . . . Not rendering evil for evil, or railing for railing: but contrariwise blessing . . . ." It is the same idea all over. The husband is not to curse his wife or rail on her, but he is to bless her. A stern warning is coupled with this command: "that your prayers be not hindered" (verse 7). This brings us to the real core of the matter of building walls with words.

SPIRITUAL WALLS

It is not only walls between one another that the Bible says we build, but walls between us and God. Our angry, cursing words toward another human being short-circuit our ability to enjoy God's fellowship and blessing. Susan Carrol had been praying for God to intervene in her marriage, but her angry words prevented her prayers from being answered. It is abundantly taught in the Scriptures that our ability to pray, have fellowship and obtain the favor of God is in direct proportion to our relationship to human beings around us. As James says, we cannot bless God and curse someone made in His image at the same time. The power of the words we speak to God are dependent upon the quality of words we say to others. Jesus said, "But if ye forgive not men their trespasses, neither will your Father forgive your trespasses" (Matthew 6:15). As long as Susan was having angry, unresolved words with her husband, it was impossible for her to get God's help in her marriage. She was not only building walls between herself and her husband, but between her and God! And while these spiritual walls cannot be seen, they are there just the same. How many people are struggling to get God's blessing while unresolved conflicts are causing them only to beat their heads against a spiritual wall of their own building!

As I flew into Belfast recently for meetings in Northern Ireland, the ugly marks of conflict were evident even before I boarded the Belfast Shuttle from London. A long chute led to the waiting room where passengers were relieved of all hand luggage before boarding the plane. The airport officials take no chances on bombs being smuggled aboard an aircraft. As I arrived in the Belfast terminal, I noticed that nobody was waiting in the terminal for incoming passengers. A message at the British Airways desk informed me that my host was waiting for me outside. As I stepped out of yet another long, walled chute outside the terminal, my host raised his camera to snap my picture. A guard yelled "No!" He explained that it was not permitted.

Bombed-out residences, stores and other buildings are everywhere. The place looks to an outsider like a city under siege. The city center is barricaded off, and all shoppers are forced to go through the endless ritual of being searched every time they enter a shop. Rows of houses are blocked up and deserted. And the walls tell the story of ugly, unfortunate barriers that are centuries old: "Up with the Provisional IRA!" "Down With Popery!" The grafitti keeps the age-old barriers of hatred alive.

While the Irish people I met everywhere were warm and wonderful, they suffer the worst sectarian barriers in the world. But the walls in Ulster are no less real than the ones we build every day with our words.

MARVELOUS OPPORTUNITY

If people can build walls with their words, they can tear them down. And one of the most life-changing things you can learn about the power of words is their power to "leap over a wall." God's people can change the world by going into the wall-wrecking business. If you would set out right now to say whatever was necessary to take down the walls separating you from others, your world would never be the same.

After all, that is what Jesus came to do: "But now in Christ Jesus ye who sometimes were far off are made nigh by the blood of Christ. For he is our peace, who hath made both one, and hath broken down the middle wall of partition between us; Having abolished in his flesh the enmity" (Ephesians 2:13-15). Jesus didn't come to build walls, but to tear them down! If His ministry has the effect of "setting at variance brother against brother," it is only because they make the choice themselves. Jesus came to reconcile the world to Himself. And we are the representatives of that reconciling ministry: "To wit, that God was in Christ, reconciling the world unto himself, not imputing their trespasses unto them; and hath committed unto us the word of reconciliation" (II Corinthians 5:19).

Let's go into the wall wrecking business.

Chapter Ten

A GIFT TO THE WORLD

Peter hung up a sign that said "Gone Fishin'." After spending three and a half years with the Lord Jesus Christ, he would resume his former occupation. But the Saviour wanted Peter to feed the world, not with fish, but with words.

Three times He asked Peter if he loved Him and three times an affirmative answer brought approximately the same response: "Feed my sheep" (John 21: 15-17). The importance of that command can hardly be overestimated.

Earlier, Jesus had stood upon a hillside and fed the multitude with loaves and fishes. After they followed Him across the sea the next day, He had told them that the real need, the real hunger could be satisfied only if they partook of *Him*! (John 6). How could that be done? So strange was this kind of talk that many of His disciples went back and did not walk with Him again. In answer to His disciples' questioning, Jesus told them He was not talking about His literal physical body, but something else. He had been talking about His spiritual nature that they must partake of if they hoped to live forever. Then He said, "The words that I speak unto you, they are spirit, and they are life" (verse 63).

When we get down to basics, there is, really, only *one* life. If the young lions get their strength from Him and the sparrow cannot fall without His permission, then Jesus is the life, and all other living things live only as they draw life from Him. The Saviour affirmed, "I am the way, the truth, and the life" (John 14:6).

If He is the life, and we are able to partake of His living, spiritual nature, how do we do it? According to the Lord Jesus, it is through His words. Doesn't the Bible say, "Man shall not live by bread alone, but by every word that proceedeth out of the mouth of God" (Matthew 4:4)? Christ is the incarnate, living Word. He imparts His life to us through His living, revealed Word. We can no more sustain our spiritual lives without His Word than we can sustain our physical lives without physical bread.

How, then, was Peter to feed Jesus' "lambs"? As the flock of God, wonderful provision has been made for us. God has provided that we should have shepherds to lead us in and out of pasture and to feed us. God's shepherds are called and appointed to feed His sheep and to look to their spiritual welfare.

In Paul's farewell address to the elders at Ephesus, we find these words: "Take heed therefore unto yourselves, and to all the flock, over the which the Holy Ghost hath made you overseers, to feed the church of God, which he hath purchased with his own blood" (Acts 20:28). It is no small responsibility to be over a flock of sheep.

To have the responsibility for the spiritual feeding of the flock of God and to provide their spiritual food is awesome. Having learned the lesson so well from his resurrected Lord, Peter cautioned the elders who would read his first epistle: "Feed the flock of God which is among you" (I Peter 5:2).

GOD'S GIFT TO THE CHURCH

Realizing the need for spiritual feeding, the Lord Jesus Christ made provision for His flock to have what they need. He called gifted and equipped men for one of the grandest occupations—preaching. Before we minimize that statement, or minimize the importance of preaching, we might consider something God says in His Word: "For the preaching of the cross is to them that perish foolishness; but unto us

which are saved it is the power of God"
(I Corinthians 1:18). There is a semi-colon
in the middle of that verse, and we need to
be careful about which side of it we put
ourselves on, because it says something
about whether we put the same importance upon this activity that God does.

How is God going to save the world? Is
He going to do it through politics, or
medicine, or entertainment? Is He going
to do it through money? Read again: "For
after that in the wisdom of God the world
by wisdom knew not God, it pleased God
by the foolishness of preaching to save
them that believe" (I Corinthians 1:21).
And Paul cautioned Timothy to keep on
preaching and feeding His flock, "For in
doing this thou shalt both save thyself,
and them that hear thee" (I Timothy 4:16).
Again, what is God's method for getting
the Word out in this present dispensation?
"But [He] hath in due times manifested
his word through preaching" (Titus 1:3).

Firm, forthright preaching is losing
popularity in our day. But God never intended that seminars, Christian literature,
devotionals, music and various other exer-
cises of our faith, important as they are,
should take the place of the God-called,
anointed preacher of the gospel. When
the Lord ascended to the Father, He gave
gifts to men that His flock may have its
needs met (Ephesians 4:8-12). And any
Christian who is not benefiting from
evangelists, pastors, teachers, etc. is miss-

ing a spiritual dimension of inestimable importance.

WHY PREACHING?

It is God's plan that the preaching of the Word, God's gift to the church, fill some important functions. We have already seen some Scriptures in which preaching is said to *save*. Preaching the Word has the power to save from the *penalty* of sin, the *power* of sin, the *preoccupation* with sin, the *presence* of sin and the *promotion* of sin. There are many instances recorded in which a preacher has come to town and preached the taverns closed, the harlots out of business, the crooked politicians out of office and left a better place for years afterward. Preaching can bring joy to a city, for sin is the thing that brings sorrow (Acts 8:5-8).

The preaching of the Word can bring strength, peace and a whole catalog of other benefits to our lives. The preacher is a special instrument, called and prepared of God, to feed His people. The reality of a group of Christians, gathering together in a body to hear a godly preacher expound the living Word of God, is an indispensable element of the Christian life.

THE GOOD NEWS

Before telephone wires were strung across the world, communications were much more cumbersome. In Bible days, the fastest means of communication was often the runner, who was trained to run for miles between stations to get a message to its destination. It was an exercise in patience. The expected recipient of a message might wait for hours until, finally, he spotted in the distance the messenger bringing the good news. It was this figure that Paul recalled as he quoted from Isaiah 52:7: "How beautiful are the feet of them that preach the gospel of peace, and bring glad tidings of good things!" (Romans 10:15). As a preacher, I can claim that verse. My wife tells me I have ugly feet, but I have chapter and verse for the fact that I have pretty feet!

It is a marvelous and reassuring fact that in this world of sorrow and gloom, God has some good news. In fact, it is the best news this world has ever heard. It is the news that death does not end it all. Man does not have to stand in judgment for his sins, for God has made a way of escape. It is the news that the burden of guilt can be removed, that the heart can, at long last, find rest in Jesus.

The word *gospel* comes from a combination of words that means "good speel," or "good news." Of all the things we have said about words, the importance of the words of the gospel overshadows them all. God has called and commissioned some men to preach, and every Christian to witness to, the most transforming words that men or angels ever dared to speak, the words of the gospel of Jesus Christ. In these words there is power to bring changes unheard of by any other means. Paul said it this way: "For I am not ashamed of the gospel of Christ: for it is the power of God unto salvation to every one that believeth; to the Jew first, and also to the Greek" (Romans 1:16).

We have harnessed the power to light up our great cities or bring them to dust. We have found the power to send man to the moon. In all of this, we have only harnessed God's power, already created into the cosmic process. But God knows only one power that can take a man from death to life, from darkness to light, from earth to Heaven—the power of the gospel!

How can such power be contained in mere words? For one thing, as we have already seen, the words of God's revealed Word all breathe the very life of the Son of God. They are living words. The gospel is the medium through which the living Spirit of God imparts life. The Bible calls this giving of spiritual life "regeneration." Call it what you like—"salvation," the "new birth"—it means the giving of a different quality of life, the eternal life found in Christ. The living words of the Scripture are like a seed—planted in a living heart they have the power to germinate faith and bring spiritual life.

Furthermore, God has a chosen way to deal with people. It is the way of faith.

Since God's spiritual blessings are not material, as mere temporal blessings are, they cannot be received by physical means. We can't back a pickup truck up to God's back door and haul them home. We can't carry them home in a bucket or a wheelbarrow. Spiritual blessings cannot be obtained through the same channels as material provision. We are only able to receive a spiritual blessing through the channel of faith.

How do we get the faith? God has provided a way: "So then faith cometh by hearing, and hearing by the word of God" (Romans 10:17). God speaks, we believe, and therefore we receive. In explaining to the Jews of his day that Abraham was saved by faith rather than by works, Paul said, "And being fully persuaded that, what he [God] had promised, he was able also to perform. And therefore it was imputed to him [Abraham] for righteousness" (Romans 4:21,22). Faith is the highest form of righteousness because it is able to lay hold of the righteousness of God. When Abraham fully believed God's promise of life and blessing, he received the imputed life and righteousness of God.

In its simplest form, the gospel is the record of the work of redemption performed in the life, death and resurrection of our Lord Jesus Christ (I Corinthians 15:1-8). He died our death that we might live. He took our place so we could avoid taking that place of judgment and suffering. He rose again that we might live forever. All our dreams and aspirations, after all, only end with the grave if there is no life in Christ. But the gospel proclaims that there is a glory and a life far beyond the grave, secured for us by the work of and in the person of Jesus Christ, the Son of God.

When we hear, or read, or somehow come into contact with the words that tell us of this grand reality, we are in the presence of the ultimate power of the universe. It is God's provision that men might receive those words into their hearts and, as a result, *live*. As incredible as it might seem, life is in a word: "Being born again, not of corruptible seed, but of incorruptible, by the word of God, which liveth and abideth forever" (I Peter 1:23).

I was something of a delinquent when I was a young man. People tried to help by a lot of means. But ten words did more for me than all the other devices anyone ever used. That was the number of words in the verse quoted to me from the Word of God that resulted in my conversion. Twenty-nine years ago, ten words cleansed my heart, gave me a new kind of life, turned my earthly life around and gave me an eternal home with God. What incredible good news!

Chapter 11

GOD'S PLANS
FOR SUCCESS

Life is not too complicated. Physically, we are what we eat. Potatoes and beans and hamburgers are the stuff our bones and muscles and organs are made of.

Spiritually and morally, we are what we ingest into our minds. Garbage in, garbage out. Whatever we feed the monster is what comes out.

The science of cybernetics has been amply explored. Our minds have been likened to a computer, responding to what we include in our programing. If we can somehow program our computer-like minds with the right goals and aspirations, the goal-seeking mechanism will simply take over, guiding us, they say, to all kinds of dizzying heights. In principle, that is a workable truth. The problem is, our computers are subject to all kinds of programing from a dozen different places at once. Sometimes this short-circuits the aparatus and leaves our goals in shambles.

But God does have a formula for thinking right in order to achieve success. And it does involve the right kind of information being fed into our minds and hearts. If we build our thoughts around the right kind of information, we will think right. If we think right, we will act right. If we act right we will be successful.

SUCCESS—WHOSE VERSION?

Before we start talking about success it needs to be established whose version of success we will use. Success can be measured by a hundred different standards. Our trouble begins when we want to define success in our own terms.

For the Christian, there can be only one definition of success—the will of God for our lives. If God is all-wise, then He knows best what is our greatest potential for living. If He is all-loving, He wants only the best for us. If He knows the end from the beginning, He can see farther than we can. His picture is bigger. Jesus was an apparent failure at the age of 33, yet here I sit two millenniums later along with a thousand others writing about Him. At the time, contemporaries might have thought an earlier young man was the real success—Alexander the Great. But the greatest Conqueror was Jesus of Nazareth.

Knowing and doing the will of God is the standard of success. The subject is taken up by Paul in his epistle to the Romans: "That ye may prove what is that good, and acceptable, and perfect, will of God" (Romans 12:1,2). What are the conditions in which we may prove, or know, the perfect will of God?

The first step is a total submission to God as a living sacrifice (Romans 12:1). This speaks for itself. The next step is this: "And be not conformed to this world: but be ye transformed by the renewing of your mind." Here, in speaking of a reshaping of our lives, the text speaks of a mind renewal, a transformation in the thinking process.

If we are going to come to the place in which we are sensitive to God's will for our lives, our minds are going to have to be changed from the usual, natural way of thinking (conformed to the world), to a new, transformed way of thinking. We are going to have to restructure our thought patterns. God has a way for us to do this.

What if you could think as God thinks? Would that bring success? Is God successful? How can we come to the place in our lives where we can think as God thinks?

The Bible reveals God's thoughts. In our quest to know the will of God, the living Words of the Scriptures are the key. Paul commanded the church at Philippi: "Let this mind be in you, which was also in Christ Jesus" (Philippians 2:5). He asked the church at Corinth: "For who hath known the mind of the Lord, that he may instruct him? But we have the mind of Christ" (I Corinthians 2:16).

The key to subjecting our thoughts to the mind and will of God is to bow our thoughts to His thoughts. It is in this way that we restructure our thoughts around His thoughts, therefore achieving success. It is not just knowing about the Word, but submitting to the Word that brings success.

Stored in the marvelous complex of our minds there are billions of impulses waiting to rise to the surface at the wink of an eye. These thoughts often betray us, even when we have the best of intentions. There is a provision God has made to help us cleanse, program and guard our minds in such a way as to guarantee success. There is a way we can be sure that our thoughts and, therefore, our actions will be in keeping with God's will.

TAKE A LESSON FROM THE COW

The cow gets to enjoy her food more than once. She eats it, spits it up a little at the time, and enjoys it again. In chewing her cud, the cow is a good example of how we can handle our spiritual food. The word "meditate" is closely akin to the word used for a cow chewing her cud. To commit the living words of the Scriptures to memory then "spit" them back up into our consciousness is God's plan for success. It is in doing this that we can restructure our thoughts around God's thoughts. We can think the way He thinks.

Both in Psalm 1:3 and in Joshua 1:8, God promises that shunning the counsel of the ungodly and meditating on the words of God's law brings unqualified success. The shepherd boy, David, sat upon the hillside and meditated upon God's law. Nine times in the Psalms he mentions this activity. When God sent His prophet, Samuel, to anoint a new king for Israel, the prophet told Jesse, David's father: "Man looketh on the outward appearance, but the Lord looketh on the heart" (I Samuel 16:7). Could it be that the constant meditation on God's Word in the night watches brought about the condition of heart God looked for in a shepherd king for Israel? Certainly it cannot be denied that the meditation paid off for us, for David produced no fewer than 73 of the sacred songs that make up the psaltery!

There is an unusual emphasis upon meditation in our day. In the kind of meditative practices based upon the Eastern mystery religions, a chant is used.

A word or group of words is chanted over and over, producing a kind of hypnotic effect upon the subject. Many devil-worshiping sects employ chants as well. But the kind of meditation taught in the Bible does not involve the chanting of a nonsense word. In order to understand Bible meditation, we have to understand the difference between our culture and that of a bygone day.

We have millions of items of information subject to instant recall because of the print, electronic and film media. Our computers are doing more of our thinking for us than ever before. But before the days of the printing press, transfer of information was a slow and laborious process. Because of this, men practiced the retention of information in their minds and passed it down to their children through word of mouth. While our present way provides for a more rapid accumulation and proliferation of knowledge, resulting in a knowledge explosion, we have suffered somewhat in our concentration. It is for this reason that many of us need to recapture the lost art of meditation.

WORDS—PEGS FOR OUR THOUGHTS

Think of words as pegs to hang thoughts on. God has given us His living Words, words to drive into our minds and fasten our thoughts. The more of His Word we can commit to our minds, the more our thoughts will be responsive to His thinking.

In order to make it easier for us, God did not hand His Word down to us in unearthly philosophic platitudes, but in simple natural figures we can understand. He set it in the enduring figure of His creation. Any of us can understand a rock, a flower, a blade of grass and a sparrow. He gave His Word to us in story form. We can relate to kings and lovers, fathers and sons.

When we fill our hearts with His Word, He gives us a thousand pictures in the galleries of our minds. We identify with His living truth as He pictures it to us in simple, ordinary figures. My favorite method for feeding my imagination upon the Word of God is to read the Bible rapidly through from start to finish, so that gradually the entire Book emerges in my mind as a complete picture of God's thinking in illustrated form. Key passages are memorized. My mind "takes a picture" of God's mind as I saturate myself with His Word.

Once our minds are saturated with His Word, our thinking can become subordinate to His thinking. Then, these words can be turned over in our thoughts, considered from different facets, and applied to our own life and situation. Whenever our thoughts would ordinarily be idle, we can turn the divine words over in our minds, actually running God's thoughts through our thoughts. This is the art of meditation: to know, to apply, to personalize, to concentrate upon God's Word.

WHAT'S IN IT FOR ME?

What can God's Word do for us? It can *cleanse* our minds, for one thing. The Word of God is likened to water: "Now ye are clean through the word which I have spoken unto you" (John 15:3). Running the clean water of God's Word through our minds is like taking a mental bath.

Meditating upon the Word of God can *structure* our minds. God always does things in an orderly, systematic way. It is a mistake to think the spiritual man is out of gear, never knowing where he is. The man who orders his thoughts according to God's thoughts is orderly in his thinking, successful in his plans.

Not only that, but he becomes successful in applying logic and clearness of thought to problem-solving. He develops a systematic approach to figuring out the knotty problems that ordinarily stump other people.

Meditation upon God's Word can *inspire* our minds. God's Word is full of ambition, valor and the fire of burning energy. The man who structures his thoughts around the mind of God is neither lethargic or lacking in energy. He is far from being lazy. The truth puts fire into our bones.

Meditation can *unclutter* our minds. When the energy of our thoughts is channeled in one direction, the deadwood has a tendency to be cleared away. One outstanding Christian leader has observed that it is impossible to think more than one thought at a time. Jesus told us that "if therefore thine eye be single, thy whole body shall be full of light" (Matthew 6:22). 6:22).

If we can let our minds be transformed by building them around the Word of God, our thoughts will become sensitive to the will of God. God's will is revealed in His Word. It reveals the kind of Person He is, how He thinks, how He acts in any given situation. God is the most successful Person there is, and in thinking like Him, therefore becoming like Him, we can achieve success beyond anything we could accomplish on our own.

Words can change your world. That is especially true if the words are the living Words of the Scriptures. The Holy Spirit works within us, using the Sword of the Spirit, the Word, to perfect in us that spiritual transformation that will make us excel: "And to know the love of Christ, which passeth knowledge, that ye might be filled with all the fulness of God. Now unto him that is able to do exceeding abundantly above all that we ask or think, according to the power that worketh in us" (Ephesians 3:19,20).

Chapter 12

THE KEY TO SELF-CONTROL

James is telling us about an exciting possibility—the possibility that if we can bring the tiny little tongue under control, we can bring our whole life under control. For those of us who have wrestled with cantankerous spirits, unkept resolutions, shattered intentions and unbridled appetites, that is a welcome idea. Is it true? Is this the key to self-control? Can you control your life by controlling your

The Key to Self-Control/121

tongue? And if so, there is the next question, Is there any way to control the tongue?

We would not want to claim more or less for the power of the tongue than the Bible does. In the "tongue chapter" (James 3), God says some pretty strong things about the tongue. It is a *fire*, it is a *defiler*, it is *set on fire of hell*, it is a *world of iniquity* (verse 6). It is *untamable*, it is *an unruly evil*, and it is *full of deadly poison* (verse 8). That's claiming a lot for this little member.

In addition, it is likened to a bit and bridle, the helm of a ship, a fountain and a fig tree. But in describing a perfect, or mature man, the Bible makes this observation: "For in many things we offend all, If any man offend not in word, the same is a perfect man, and able also to bridle the whole body" (James 3:2). Here is one area of our lives we can work on, because God says it will bring multiplied results. If we can learn to control this little nuisance, we can take care of the rest!

We have already spoken of some ways that will help tame the tongue. To realize the vast potential of words for good or evil and our corresponding responsibility is one healthy step. The right kind of prayer life is a tongue tamer. It is hard to talk about somebody if you are praying for him! Exposure to and meditation upon the Scriptures is another way to tame the tongue. Furthermore, just to realize that all our words are being recorded in Heaven is enough to make us stop before we speak.

THE RUDDER AND THE BIT

In comparing the tongue with the bit in a horse's mouth, or the steering apparatus of a boat, God's Word is indirectly pointing to the power of the tongue to provide direction for our lives. I would like to suggest some ways this can be done. We can use the tongue to send our lives in the wrong direction as well, but we will focus on the positive side.

The tongue can direct our lives through *commitment*. Our thoughts are private property, but as soon as we verbalize a plan or course of action, we involve others. In making a commitment, we set certain forces in action that can strengthen our plans. We can remain very timid about a plan of action, but the act of committing ourselves by saying what we intend to do gives firmness and reinforcement to those ideas.

Once our plans are out in the open, we cannot be as apathetic about them as before, since an open commitment makes them concrete. It puts us in a place in which there is pressure on us to follow through. This is the reason so few of us want to make a commitment. Instinctively, we realize it will force us to take action.

All of us can remember things we

thought of and dreamed about doing for a period of time without ever getting around to it until we shared it with others and they encouraged us to go ahead. Commitment is a powerful principle. Who cannot remember the sense of finality and dread that accompanied the public commitment of our faith in Christ? But once done, our faith and life were greatly strengthened. Our whole system of making a public appeal in the revival meeting or evangelistic service is designed to bring a person out, to direct him to a course of action, to make a commitment.

Most of us never get going on a thing until we commit ourselves. We might visualize what we want to do and never get around to doing it because we do not verbalize it. How many potential acts of greatness have been lost for a lack of commitment! But to say, "I am going to do it!" puts steam into our plans. Prayerful commitment is like turning the horse or steering the ship in its proper direction. You have to start in order to reach your destination, and the act of commitment is a way of steering our lives in the right direction. The alternative is terrible. It is like foundering on a troubled sea without a rudder. "Commit thy works unto the Lord, and thy thoughts shall be established" (Proverbs 16:3).

Bridles and helms are used not only to commit us to a certain direction, but also to *correct our course*. This is another valuable use of the tongue. Janie Green had said something in a moment of anger that set her whole family in an uproar. She knew that it had resulted in making her miserable, and others, too. But Janie could not bring herself to say the words that would have straightened the thing out. Just a few words would have corrected her course and helped others, too. Most people, with a few phone calls or visits and a few well-chosen words, could correct grievous problems in their lives.

THE FOUNTAIN

The next figure James uses is that of a fountain: "Doth a fountain send forth at the same place sweet water and bitter?" (James 3:11). The writer of the Proverb says, "The words of a man's mouth are as deep waters, and the wellspring of wisdom as a flowing brook" (Proverbs 18:4).

Knowing some things about a fountain can help us with the tongue. One of the first things we observe is that the kind of water inside will be the kind that comes out. That is James' whole point. You can't go to a salt water fountain and get a drink of fresh water. One of the first rules in controlling the tongue is to have the right kind of stuff on the inside. In fact, if you want to know what is inside a person, just listen to what comes out.

You may want to know, "What kind of person am I?" The tongue will tell. Our words sort of turn us inside out, showing the whole world what's on the inside. If you find your words offending people, costing you friends, lacking in spiritual power, the answer is not to trade in your tongue for a new model. The tongue only obeys. It only speaks what the heart tells it to speak. Cleverness and deception may hide the truth for awhile, but the tongue is a dreadful tattletale. It will eventually let the world know what kind of person its owner is. It reveals what we are. And what we are is infinitely more important than what we pretend to be.

Another thing about a fountain is its vulnerability to pollution. It only takes a little bit of poison to ruin the whole supply. I grew up drinking sulfur water from artesian wells. Being used to it, I rather enjoyed it. But my friends visiting from other places only needed to smell it to know something was amiss. Likewise, the trained ear can tell immediately, as soon as we open our mouths, if there is something wrong, something poison in the fountain of our hearts.

James spoke about a strange occurrence: "Therewith bless we God, even the Father; and therewith curse we men, which are made after the similtude of God. Out of the same mouth proceedeth blessing and cursing. My brethren, these things ought not so to be. Doth a fountain send forth at the same place sweet water and bitter?" (James 3:9-11). James was observing that he could tell something was wrong with the fountain by the kind of water that was coming out. We might be blessing God, but if we are cursing men, there is poison at the source.

Talking bitterly about others, making ourselves look big at their expense, criticizing them unnecessarily—are all indications of something wrong with the spirit. The tongue, therefore, becomes a valuable aid to us. It is like an indicator on the dashboard of an automobile. It lets us know if there's trouble on the inside. It's like a red flag that says, "Warning, spiritual danger!" The tongue probes the deep recesses of the soul, dredging out the spiritual mud and putting it on the outside where it can be seen.

One other thing about a fountain. James recognized only two kinds of water—good and bad. If we stay with his idea, there are only two kinds of speech. If our speech is not honoring the Lord or blessing others,it is dishonoring to God. Jesus told us "every idle word" would be brought into judgment.

In James 3:14-16, we find these comments: "But if ye have bitter envying and strife in your hearts, glory not, and lie not against the truth. This wisdom descendeth not from above, but is earthly, sensual, devilish. For where envying and strife is, there is confusion and every evil work." Envying and strife, revealed by the tongue, calls for another danger flag.

Somebody is troubling the water; and it's not the Holy Spirit. Never mind saying we are just "standing up for our rights." James says, "glory not, and lie not against the truth" (verse 14). The signal says, "Danger: devil at Work!" If this type of spirit is evident in our conversation, we can always be sure it is an attack of Satan. It's time to pray, confess and get right. The tongue will tell.

FIGS AND OLIVE BERRIES

The third figure James uses is that of a fruitbearing plant. Whatever you plant, that's what you get. James asks, "Can the fig tree, my brethren, bear olive berries? Either a vine, figs?" (James 3:12). The writer of Hebrews calls our praise to God, "the fruit of the lips." And Proverbs 18:20 declares, "A man's belly shall be satisfied with the fruit of his mouth; and with the increase of his lips shall he be filled." So the Bible is telling us that the words we speak are the fruit of a lifetime. So strong is this idea that Proverbs 18:21 tells us, "Death and life are in the power of the tongue: and they that love it shall eat the fruit therof."

Our words can reflect the fruit of the Spirit: "love, joy, peace, long-suffering, gentleness, goodness, faith, meekness, temperance" (Galatians 5:22,23). This is the kind of fruit the world is starved for. This kind of fruit is in great demand. If your lips will bear *this* fruit, you will never lack companionship or blessing.

Our words can reflect a bitter fruit. "The root of the righteous yieldeth fruit," says Proverbs 12:12. The *root* determines the *fruit.* If there is a "root of bitterness" (Hebrews 12:15) in the heart, the fruit will be bitter.

Our words can reflect a heart of praise: "By him therefore let us offer the sacrifice of praise to God continually, that is, the fruit of our lips giving thanks to his name" (Hebrews 13:15). Can we give God a basket of fruit that will please Him? Yes, the fruit of our lips. He knows very well that when our hearts are thankful they are in good condition.

Our lips can utter the fruit of righteousness: "But the wisdom that is from above is first pure, then peaceable, gentle, and easy to be intreated, full of mercy and good fruits, without partiality, and without hypocrisy. And the fruit of righteousness is sown in peace of them that make peace" (James 3:17,18). Peace is included in the cluster of the fruit of the Spirit. As a child of God, I want to sow righteousness. God says that fruit cannot be sown in an atmosphere of strife and conflict, but only in peace. We are trees, and our words are the fruit. "By their fruits," Jesus said, "ye shall know them" (Matthew 7:20).

"Out of the abundance of the heart the mouth speaketh" (Matthew 12:34).